REQUIEM
BOOK 1: ORIGINS

TAVEYAH LaSHAY

TAVEYAHLASHAY.COM

Copyright © 2019 Taveyah LaShay.

The right of Taveyah LaShay to be identified as the author of this work has been asserted.

All rights reserved.

No part of this book may be reproduced, stored in a retrieval system, or transmitted, in any form, or by any means (electronic, mechanical, photocopying, recording or otherwise) without the prior written permission of the author, except in cases of brief quotations embodied in reviews or articles. It may not be edited, amended, lent, resold, hired out, distributed or otherwise circulated, without the publisher's written permission.

Permission can be obtained from www.taveyahlashay.com

This book is a work of fiction. Except in the case of historical fact, names, characters, places, and incidents either are products of the author's imagination or are used fictitiously. Any resemblance to actual persons, living or dead, events, or locales is entirely coincidental.

ISBN: 978-1-7340120-0-2

Published by Taveyah LaShay

Cover design & interior formatting:
Mark Thomas / Coverness.com

PRAISE FOR

REQUIEM
BOOK 1: ORIGINS

… an amazing book and read. I'm telling all my friends and followers to go check her out. Taveyah LaShay is a great writer and beautiful soul. …

-R Braxton, Tampa, FL

Requiem definitely was a great read. Full of suspense and had me breaking my 2 chapters a night rule due to my busy schedule. It was to hard to put it down. I can't wait to read more!

-S. Peterson- Milwaukee, WI

This book is a AWESOME read!!! Definitely a page turner that will have you wondering what is next. Suspense, curiosity, sex appeal all rolled up in one!!! I can't wait for the next Saga of this book!!

-C. Davis - Tampa, FL

I couldn't put the book down, I was engaged and looking forward to reading about the next character. The book made me feel like I was one of the characters. It kept me ensnared, laughing, crying and falling in love with the characters all over again

-T. Hancock - Tampa, FL

I absolutely loved it! This book was full of drama, suspense and very emotional! The narration was outstanding and gave the story that extra flair! It will keep you entertained! The author did an amazing job with the character builds and plot! This was my first book by this author but definitely not my last.

-G.C.

Dedication

*I dedicate this book to the night time hours of 8-2.
Without you, none of this would be possible.*

Requiem *(n.)* – an act or token of remembrance

PREFACE

Every tragedy has its origin. And this one is no different. It starts with an inseparable bond between cousins who grew up more like sisters. Annemarie and McKenzie did everything together. As young girls, when they weren't in school, singing in the church choir, or running the Jupiter dirt roads to the water banks for turtle eggs to sell, they filled their time braiding each other's long thick hair on their grandmother's shotgun smoking porch planning to share their future. They wanted to go to the same schools, drive the same cars, get married on the same day to brothers, and would make an exception for cousins, so they would never be too far apart. They even wanted to have home births and have their babies share the same birth date. So far, everything that they had planned for came true.

West Tampa, winter 1987, now both twenty-five, they lay in adjacent rooms, in their grandmother's shotgun home, fighting for their lives and the lives of their firstborn, with only the help of their midwives to assist them through the cold and the pain. Their husbands who were both away in Uncle Sam's war were brothers and weren't due to come home for at least another three months. They could hear each other's moans of agony and pain echoing through their grandmother's house as they were directed and coaxed to push through the ring of fire. The pinewood shiplap in the old house seemed to inhale and exhale with each contraction. The birthing process felt like forever before two new sharp cries echoed off the walls. Even though exhausted, Annemarie was eager to check on her cousin so they could share their newfound joys and feed their newborns together. She had her midwife assist her to the wooden wheelchair that her husband Verdell, had made her before he left. Placing a baby in each arm, Annemarie rolled down the hall, anxious to tell McKenzie about her twins. But the closer the midwife pushed her to McKenzie's closed door, she began to panic. Once in the room, instantly, Annemarie sensed something was wrong. She didn't hear a baby. Only hers were cooing. Through the weak firelight, she saw a baby lying flat on her cousin's exposed breasts, eyes wide facing her, so she could see the death that swam in them. Annemarie searched her cousin's face for confirmation of the terribleness that she already knew in her heart. McKenzie let out a low and gut pulling roar that seemed to shake the room. Her midwife rushed over to take the stillborn. McKenzie fought to keep the baby in her arms, using the warmth from her body attempt to wake him. When that didn't work, she tried to feed him. His body remained limp and unresponsive. Now in tears herself, Annemarie looked at her own two baby boys. She knew right away what she had to do. She grabbed one and placed it on McKenzie's chest and nuzzled the other to her own. At first, McKenzie turned her face away, not touching the newborn on her chest. The warm and squirming little body grabbed at a long braided plat that hung down in McKenzie's face and tried to nurse the end. The light in McKenzie's eyes brightened a little as she looked down to see Annemarie's baby laying on her chest. His toffee color, full head of slick black hair, and almond-shaped eyes looked very similar to her features. Quickly glancing at Annemarie, McKenzie was confused at the beautiful baby boy on her chest and the other baby boy, who was just as handsome, if not more, in her cousin's arms. Annemarie quickly explained that God blessed her with a baby for each of them, that she had not fed him yet, and if McKenzie wanted a baby, he was as good as hers. With both men off at war, Annemarie needed to spare her cousin from heartache. What harm could there be in giving a twin and keeping the secret? She and Verdell couldn't afford two, and she couldn't stand to see her favorite cousin, her sister, in despair. The boys were fraternal and wouldn't be hard to play off as cousins she reasoned. One brown-skinned the other just a tad darker. They only shared a birthmark shaped like a crescent moon, no bigger than her thumb, at the nape of their necks. As the boys got older, there were none the wiser, but as secrets do, they began to eat at the soul. Known or not, the essence of it seeps in and devours everything that is good until it is all only a triggered memory.

CHAPTER 1

VERDELL

The arches in Verdell's feet stung, and his calves burned as he bent down low to shuffle backward down the court. At the age of eighteen, his 6'2" broad, lean, and milk chocolate brown athletic frame was in better shape than most rookie basketball players. And true to form, he was playing this game like a Division I starter destined for the big league. Staying close enough to the ball for a steal, but not close enough to foul was just one of the skills that he had mastered over his past four years of high school ball and during the three years prior in AAU.

"Move out the way pussy," DJ barked as he drove the ball hard down the middle of the court stopping right inside the three-point line just as Verdell used his body to cut him off. Verdell could read every play that DJ had. He schooled him on most of them. Verdell anticipated DJ's drive to the paint and was careful not to foul him as DJ faked the ball left and then back out to Yellow Jacket's power forward, Dusty Hawkins. Dusty had a pretty good lift from the three-point line, so Verdell made sure to keep his defense tight and stayed in Dusty's face. This Verdell knew because he saw him play before and now he had just witnessed firsthand his team murdered in the last three quarters. Dusty hit eleven three's in three quarters, keeping the score between the rivals very close. Verdell wasn't going to give Dusty that chance again especially, not this close to the 4th quarter. "Zone D!!," Coach Shepard yelled across the court signaling for the Terrier's defense to back off from man to man and defend their respective zones of the court. But not Verdell, he didn't need the coach to tell him where he needed to be on defense. The man to man press was mandatory and seemed to be working so far.

"Terrier's senior #28, Verdell Hamilton, putting the pressure on thick for this Yellow Jacket offense. Let's see if DJ Hamilton can get himself out of this one before the shot clock runs out." Making eye contact, Verdell gave DJ a little smirk through his mouth guard. Bouncing the ball and looking past Verdell to briefly scan the court, Verdell could feel a heatwave of hatred radiate from DJ as he debated his next move. But Verdell didn't need time to think he knew when to make his move. And he was going to take this opportunity to show DJ the hard way why those who thought long, thought wrong. Verdell knew he had to move quickly. From his peripheral, he saw his teammate Bobby "Dunkem" Vincent, slowly creeping up on his right toward the backcourt with his right arm extended as he mouthed what appeared to be "ball" over and over again.

"Time to school YO' ass, pussy," Verdell managed to shout through the mouth guard as he caught DJ in mid dribble and pushed the ball right through his hands. The stands went crazy. In two long strides, Verdell had control of the ball and launched it down the court for the fast break to Bobby. At only 5'9", Bobby was the best dunker in the county and made sure to let everyone know it every chance he got. At the park; at practice; in the school hallways; in the classroom, anything that looked like a rim was getting dunked in. As long as Verdell had known "Dunkem," he always talked about how he wanted to dunk the ball so hard that it would break the glass. Even though he never made it happen before, tonight's game had sparked enough electricity and ego to make this the one night to never say never. Bobby caught the ball with his outstretched and waiting hand just as he stepped to the three-point line and then tipped it back to Verdell at the corner of the foul line. Verdell floated the ball back up as Bobby launched off his soles and flew through the air catching the ball and slamming it into the hoop. The play ran like one fluid motion.

"Yoooooooooooo" Verdell hollered and cackled as Bobby gave out a resounding roar and hung on the rim a little too long after the ref's whistle had blown. Dunkem landed so hard on his feet that Verdell could have sworn he felt the ground shake. The crowd and the announcers went wild.

"You just witnessed it here, folks. Terrier's seniors #32,

Bobby "Dunkem" Vincent, with the slam dunk and #28 Verdell Hamilton with the steal and assist. We got a game here, folks. Two minutes eight seconds, fourth quarter, Terriers 67, Yellow Jackets 65." The stands whooped, booed, and screamed for their sons, nephews, cousins, friends, and classmates. The gymnasium was in an uproar. Somewhere, in the back of the stands, a shouting match of "0 Five" was being had by the senior classmen. The resounding noise echoed around the space.

Alerted by the newly excited crowd, the uniformed TPD officers spread throughout the gym on standby to spring into action if things got too out of control. But nothing less could be expected of the rival teams, especially during the last game of the season and the final game for the seniors.

*

After this, they would all go off to work in their family's businesses, go to serve their country, go to college, or fall into whatever the cold hardened streets had to offer. As for Verdell, he couldn't wait to go to college. He had been working with his father all year and the previous summer doing all kinds of odd and end jobs to save for the small apartment he found just a few blocks from the University of South Florida. He hadn't told his girlfriend Missy about it yet but, he couldn't wait to surprise her with the news at graduation. Unlike some of the other boys on his team, Verdell enjoyed school and wanted to be more than the next NBA legend. He had received several scholarships for both his academic and athletic ability from several schools around the country for his 3.9 GPA and state championships, but Verdell chose USF. Not only did it provide him an opportunity to stay close to home and Missy, who was also going to USF to study medicine and become a Pediatrician, but it allowed him to pursue his dream of studying botany and playing at a Division I school. Basketball was his second love. It was one of those things pushed on him by his alcoholic father at a young age, who was desperate to win a bet that he was too intoxicated to do himself. Being shook from sleep in the dead of night and drug to the homemade wicker laundry basketball goal in the alley behind their home, became a series of years of his father's Hail Mary attempt to win back bill or rent money that had been gambled away earlier that night at some hole in the wall. Rather than being upset at his father for dragging him out of bed on those late school nights, he waited for it, even anticipated it. It seemed to be the only time he made his father proud and always welcomed the sour smell, gruff voice, and tug on his pajama collar as a chance to continue to do so. Sometimes the men he had to play against were more than four times his age, but they were usually just as hammered as his father, if not more, and made them easy wins. Those were great times, at least until his father's drinking and gambling made his mother sick to death and took their family down a path that, on many occasions, Verdell forced himself to forget.

*

Verdell's sole focus on DJ made him miss the play that was in motion. He ran face-first into Teddy Roads, who had set a pick for him and who exaggeratedly slid from the free-throw line to just under the basket and rolled over on his back into the stands. "What a crab!" Verdell thought out loud as he watched the ogre make an ass of himself flying across the court. Like anyone would even believe he had been bumped that hard. Verdell knew what kind of showman Teddy was from their AAU days. From where he stood, he could see that nothing had changed. The ref blew one short chirp through his whistle.

"Foul! Terriers #28, Yellow Jackets ball."

"Man, that's bullshit!" Verdell heard himself scream a little too close to the ref before he had a chance to think otherwise. As if on cue, the coach called a timeout right before the referee could blow his whistle for the technical. Another foul was the last thing Verdell needed and so was giving a free shot to the other team. Making a point to jog slower than the rest of the team back to the Terrier's bench, Verdell knew he was falling apart out there. The coach was going to have his ass for it.

Sure enough, "Get your ass over here Hamilton and sit your ass down. I don't know what the hell you got going on out there, but you better get your head out of your ass and back in this game."

Too embarrassed at coach's truth and ashamed of his performance, Verdell couldn't open his mouth to respond. Instead, he bit the inside of his cheek, despite the bulky mouth guard, and nodded his head.

"Chirp, chirp" sounded the referee's whistle to signal the end of the timeout.

"Terriers 67. Yellow Jackets 65. Only one minute and five seconds left in the fourth quarter folks. Terrier's star point, Verdell Hamilton has four fouls, twenty-three points, eight assists, five rebounds. The game is too close to call. Both teams are going to have to kick it up one helluva notch to get a chance at that trophy."

"Don't fuck this up! Don't fuck this up!" is all Verdell could think as he walked back into the game, shaking the tingling from his fingertips.

The pressure of the game had always sent a charge through him, and he gladly welcomed it. Verdell's earlier foul had put the ball in play on the offense's side of the court and unfortunately at a disadvantage for his team. Verdell knew he had little chance of stopping the ball but, that didn't mean he wasn't going to make them fight for it though. Waving his hands wildly in front of Teddy's face, who was DJ's obvious choice since that was his go-to guy on an out of bounds play, Verdell made the mistake of keeping his back to the ball for two seconds too long. No sooner than DJ tossed in the ball, Dusty Hawkins came out of nowhere through the crowd of defenders, to catch the inbound pass. Dusty quickly threw the ball back to DJ, who went in for a left-hand finger roll layup that would have been butter, if the ball would have found the hoop instead of circling the rim. Finally catching up to the play, Verdell blew out a breath of relief for the missed shot and went in for the rebound at the same time as DJ and two other Yellow Jackets. They all jumped once, twice, and the third time DJ's elbow found its way into the soft space below Verdell's diaphragm, right before the ball finally fell off the side of the hoop.

Verdell bit down on his mouth guard in pain and tried to shake off the blow. But that was before DJ came down with the ball swinging his elbows, catching the already unstable Verdell with another sharp hit to the rib cage making him gasp for air before he fell onto the court and slid out of bounds. This game was going to be the last one of the season. The last one of his high school career and Verdell couldn't go out like this and let his cousin get away with his bullshit. Family or not, this rivalry had gone on long enough, even if the ref didn't call the foul.

*

As boys, when their drunken fathers pit them against each other for gambling debts and simple bets, Verdell could remember the games turning into boxing matches because neither he nor DJ could stand to disappoint their father. When Verdell would come in the house with his face scarred and bruised, his mother would get a hot rag and press it to his face. She would tell him in a voice as sweet as sugar, "You boys are all just different sides of the same coin that won't spend on nothing." Even though it had already been eight years since his mother died, Verdell remembered the saying but still didn't know what she meant by it. His mother could never understand why his father and his uncle had to drag their children into their dick measuring matches. From the time they were old enough to stand to pee, everything between he and DJ had been a battle. Being the same age, similar to their father's, didn't make it any better. When puberty broke out, it was who had the most hair down there and whose skin complexion was smoother than chocolate instead of pickled like cucumbers. As they grew up, it turned into whose hair had more waves than the ocean and whose pecker could pee the farthest. It was always something. Basketball was the first thing that they seemed to be evenly matched at because it required pure talent. And Verdell had plenty of talent. His uncle Dhorian and his father had fallen out a long time ago because uncle Dhorian had to remind them all that he was a self-made man while his dad Verdell Sr., was a pushover who hauled other people's garbage. Dhorian Junior must have soaked that shit in after all these years, and Verdell was feeling very tempted to knock his ass off that pedestal.

*

The loud boos and jeers from the fans resounded like a buzzing hive and right about now he was feeling the sting. Verdell shook his head in an attempt to bring everything back into focus. The pressure of their possible loss angered and embarrassed him. Verdell's face flushed as he attempted several times to push up on his wrists to stand and get back in the game.

"Yo, that's real fucked up DJ" he hissed, before sucking in a big breath of air to help him get through the pain to his feet. He moved his tongue around his mouth and tasted blood, which had to come from his split lip compliments of DJ's elbow.

Spitting out the blood from his cut lip, Verdell yelled, "That last foul was bullshit!" And he knew the refs saw it, so why was there no call? Verdell finally made it steadily to his feet when he felt a hand on his back.

Before he could grab what he thought was a helping hand, he heard DJ's voice, "You gonna lay there dead like your momma, or you gonna man up and catch the last thrity seconds of this ass whooping?" At the mention of his mother, Verdell knew that DJ knew he was going to hit a nerve. He never thought his cousin, his first cousin at that, could have ever said anything so black-hearted to him.

*

Ever since his mother passed, his love for basketball was used as a crutch to keep him going and refocus his energy. He missed seeing her smiling face in the stands, even after all these years. He continued because he knew she wanted the best for him, to see him be somebody great. And to achieve the kind of greatness he wanted to brag to her about in his prayers, he needed to play his heart out tonight in front of this crowd filled with USF talent scouts like his life depended on it. But getting a scout's attention and pursuing any future with basketball was now out the window.

*

Shaking off the swirling haze that had overcome his entire being just one minute earlier, Verdell, now filled with a bubbling rage, moved quicker than DJ expected and slapped him with an open hand right in his mouth. The attempts made by the coaches, the refs, and his teammates to get Verdell cool and off the court were all phased out in slow motion.

"Fuck you, DJ. Talk about my mother, what the fuck is wrong with your stupid ass?"

Verdell's booming voice could have been heard in the next county over, and he wouldn't have given a damn. He was tired of DJ's shit. He was sick of being punked and turning the other cheek. He was upset that his mother would never be with him again. She would usually be the one to talk him out of character decisions like these. His father could care less about his character as long as he was winning.

While DJ was holding his now swelling jaw, Verdell punched him in the stomach and kicked him in his back, making sure to connect and push off with all the weight that his leg could muster, as he dropped to the floor. In that next moment, TPD wrestled Verdell to the ground and now had him held up in a part of the locker room separated from the rest of the world. Even with his uncle threatening to press charges against him, his coach screaming about how his bright future was now a waste, and his wino of a father not picking up the phone, Verdell felt like a weight had finally come off his shoulders. At least he had his pride. The only thing that could have made this night better was if he could have whooped DJ's ass and won the game.

CHAPTER 2

MADISIN

"Now you know I love you, Maddie. It's just not the right time for us to let everyone know we're together." Paul whispered into Madisin's ear as he released her from the sloppy kisses he placed on her lobe.

Madisin had heard that line from him before and knew that it only came from a makeup session between him and his Muppet of a wife. Just three weeks before he swore they were going to run away together and that he would gladly give up his waterfront home on Bay Shore Blvd, his wife, and her old money, his brat of a child if it would make her happy. But then again, he was waist-deep inside her when he said that. It never failed, here they were, him trying to swirl his fingers around in her honeypot to the same tune. She hoped he was too busy licking and kissing her neck to see the look on her face. It was quickly turning from one of passion and horniness to disgust. After being Paul's secretary and mistress for the past eleven years and giving him a beautiful daughter, she thought he would have come to his senses and came up with something better than "it's not the right time" by now. It was just so selfish of him to think that she would continue to settle for the lavish life and great sex that he provided her without access to what she wanted. Him. That is all she really wanted. Well, that and the great sex.

Paul took Madisin's face in his hands, ignoring her blank gaze and stiff neck, and licked his thick tongue around her lips before forcing it inside her mouth. Madisin resisted the urge to push him away. She barely got a chance to spend any time with him over the past few months. Plus, she did not want to argue over that or his wife. That was not how she wanted to spend her off-hours. Paul must have realized that his kisses were a dud at that moment and trailed his slippery tongue from Madisin's pursed lips down her cheek to the dip in her neck.

"Damn him," Madisin thought as chills ran from her spine and created butterflies in her stomach. He knew that her neck made her weak every time. Paul roughly turned her around and pushed her face down with her lace-covered breasts pressed flat on his lacquered wood mahogany desk. Unzipping his pants and grinding his growing manhood on her plump peach-shaped behind, Madisin faked a protest, raising the tone of her voice to that of a Betty Boop sound alike, "Mr. Christen!" But her mocked innocence was cut short by Paul's husky fore and middle fingers being maneuvered into her mouth, immediately shushing her. Paul liked it when Madisin role played for him. He loved it when she sucked on his fingers, especially when they had her juices on them. Madisin swirled her tongue up and down each finger, slowly flicking it in the dip between each member. She slurped and sucked them as if his other member was in her hot and moist mouth, instead of just his thick and stubby fingers. When she sucked his middle finger back to her uvula, Madisin exaggerated the gagging noise just a little, for his benefit. He also loved it when she gagged.

"I told you to call me Paul," Paul tried to say in a tone meant to chastise but came out more like a whimper of pleasure.

If she didn't know any better, Madisin would think he was about to bust his load already. Using his free hand, Paul slid his cowhide belt slowly through the loop of his slacks and spanked Madisin hard on her ass with the leather. Madisin jumped in pleasure, always surprised at how the pain made her so wet between her thighs. However, she hoped he would hurry up and get on with it.

*

Lately, he seemed to like taking his time enjoying her, and she wanted to love every minute of it, but the new setting for their rendezvous had now become his home office instead of their usual meeting spot at the Lodge. It just made her so nervous being so close to his family. As bad as Madisin wanted Paul, that was not to be confused with her wanting his house or his bratty kid. He could keep his family, but Madisin wanted him to come with her so they could start their own lives. But being as resistant as he had been to hear her out recently, she held a bit of information that would push him to make a choice a lot sooner than later.

*

Paul smacked the leather against her already tender brown ass again, bringing Madisin back from her roaming thoughts. Paul pressed his stiff shaft into her as he slid his cold hands up her legs and under her dress. The throaty chuckle that slipped from his mouth let Madisin know that he was pleased to see that she followed his instructions to the letter. No panties and no rug. She giggled as his fingers thoroughly explored and inspected her wetness. A gasp escaped her as he slid his fingers right into her center. He knew her body so well. It was like a second sense that he knew just how long and how deep to pound her mound whether it was with his fingers, his thick shaft, or his tongue. This man knew what he was doing. Madisin couldn't deny it was part of the reason why she stayed as a willing participant in their eleven-year affair. Paul pulsed his fingers together slow and deep, making sure to press against the top left corner of Madisin's walls, making her blow out soft puffs of air as she whimpered and moaned. Paul swept Madisin's curly light brown hair from her shoulders to kiss her neck and whisper nasty nothings in her ear.

"MMMMM," Paul growled. "You smell so damn good." His warm breath and lips on her skin made her cream rain down on his fingers. Slowly rising off his members to face him, Madisin wasn't giving in so easy.

"Shut up and make me cum already." When Paul started unzipping his slacks, Madisin wagged a finger in his face and with one hand on his shoulders pushed him to his knees. Hopping up on Paul's desk, Madisin leaned back on her elbows and with her legs squeezed tightly together, lifted them straight in the air, exposing only the glistening flesh of her swollen clit.

"If you think I smell that good, maybe you should taste me too." Spreading her legs as far apart to the East and the West of the room's compass, Madisin seductively bit her lip and watched Paul's eyes glaze with desire. Motioning for him to come closer, Paul opened his mouth, exposing his thick pink tongue and moved in closer towards the center of Madisin's gaping legs. Feeling the warmth of his entire tongue on her clit made her head fall back and her breath catch in her throat. Paul began to move his head in sync to the steady rhythm of Madisin's hips, eagerly pumping against his face. She found it hard to keep her moans stifled with all of Paul's slurping as he forced his tongue inside her repeatedly.

In one swift motion, Paul wrapped his lips around the hood of Madisin's clit and sucked her jewel into his hot and moist mouth. The cold pressure that started to chill in Madisin's toes moved up to her spine, made her back arch, and her soul moan.

"Oh, God, Paul! Oh, shit. Baby, please. Damn. Oh, my God! I need a minute." Madisin thought the pause Paul gave her would give her time to recover when he released her clit. But

Paul's husky voice and the strength of his arms as he pulled her ass off of his desk and closer to his face made her shutter and damn near choke.

"You were right baby. You do taste good." Caught off guard, Madisin coughed to clear the dry air from her throat and regained her composure enough to mention how her wet ass being drug across an unfinished wood table would cause chaffing. When Paul didn't respond, Madisin looked up at Paul and caught a glimpse of the predator in his eyes.

She loved that he still carried that hunger for her. Before Madisin could ask him where he got the chair that he was sitting in and seemed to appear out of nowhere, Paul had pounced and was back to devouring her hotbox like it was his last meal. By the time Paul finished, he had needed more than a dinner napkin to clean his face. He had sucked her until she was dry and licked her walls until she was wet again. Paul slurped her like she had all thirty-one flavors of Baskin Robbins inside of her and he wasn't stopping until he had tried them all.

Picking his discarded dress shirt off the floor and using it to wipe her juices off of his face, Madisin stared at Paul until their eyes locked. He had to love her, Madisin thought. Nobody licks you that good and doesn't love you. Standing from his plush brown leather chair, Paul grabbed Madisin by the hand and sat her up on his desk. Placing a hand behind her head, he kissed Madisin deeply. Already drunk with lust and the hunger for more, Madisin reached into Paul's slacks and met a very eager rock hard shaft. She gripped it and began to move her hand up and down its long thick ridges.

"You're so beautiful. I don't know what I would do without my chocolate."

Madisin immediately tensed at his words about "his chocolate." It was ironic that he loved her skin, but would not acknowledge his own. His skin had an olive hue that contrasted with his red hair, deep brown eyes, thick lips, and a subtle full nose. She didn't know how he was still in hiding after all this time. How others didn't see it. Madisin was jolted back to the passion of the moment when she felt Paul plunge his swollen penis inside of her. Her moans quickly escalated to cries of pleasure. Gasping and grabbing at the corners of the desk, Madisin knew she was going to need to hold on for this ride. Paul lifted his leg onto the table and pulled hard and slow with both hands at Madisin's waist so that she slammed back into him with each thrust, prepping her body to receive all of him.

"Oh my God Paul! Go faster," Madisin whined. Paul sped up and gripped one hand on Madisin's shoulder to give them both leverage, arching Madisin's back. "Yes, yes, yes. Don't stop. Please don't stop" Paul was like a turbo drill, pounding her box mercilessly as he grasped at her hair, neck, and waist in an attempt to control the heat steadily rising in him. Madisin felt herself flush cold and her body begin to erupt when Paul snatched himself from her and picked her up supporting her still parted legs and back placing her atop the leather chair he had just occupied.

Paul ran his tongue on her lips and flitted it across her tongue as Madisin opened her mouth to receive his kisses. Paul thrust himself back into her moistness, still slurping on Madisin's lips. The room was starting to spin. The sex had always been great with Paul, but he felt different. He was more passionate, doing everything he knew she loved, and it was beginning to feel like too much for Madisin to bear. She had to remind herself to breathe. She didn't realize she had been holding her breath until her legs stopped trembling, her eye stopped twitching, and she sucked all of the available air in the room into her lungs.

Breathing heavy and rubbing his nose against hers, Paul asked, "You okay baby?

Madisin gave out a burst of laughter, "I should be the one asking that question Mr. Christen. If I didn't know any better, I would say that you had a point to prove."

Paul laughed too, "I always have a point to prove."

Madisin took his response as the perfect opening for what she wanted to discuss. Sliding her drained and sweat ravaged body off of his desk, Madisin walked over to him and started helping him get a new starched shirt and cufflinks out of his closet.

"Baby," Madisin began slowly "you don't have to prove yourself to me. I know who you are."

Bending down to kiss her forward, "I know you do baby. That's why I love you." Paul crossed his office and walked towards the bathroom. Exasperated that he hadn't caught on to her I know who you are comment, she decided to be a little more forward.

"Well if you love me, Paul, come be with me, come be with our daughter. No one will look at you differently for being with your own kind." She could see Paul's demeanor change as he stiffened, and she tried not to appear too anxious for his response and shifted her gaze from his visage looming in the bathroom doorway. Paul absently adjusted the knot in his tie as he fixed the emptiness in his eyes on her.

Slowly walking over toward Madisin, Paul shrugged his shoulders and repeated her pointed comment as a question. "Humph, my own kind, huh?"

It was something about the way he said it that made Madisin uneasy. In their time together, she had never heard him speak in such a distant and sarcastic tone, and it was in contrast to everything the last twenty minutes had shown. As he approached, her uncertainty of Paul's next move made her back away.

"What do you mean by that?" Paul questioned and stopped just within arm's length of Madisin. She found herself backed into the corner of his built-in mahogany bookshelf that she had ordered herself to match the rest of the office furniture. Wasn't this ironic.

Attempting to cover the mounting fear in her voice, "I only mean that you would be more at peace and happier when you don't have to hide certain things…"

The backhand came quicker than Madisin could move. Her ears registered the sound before her face felt the sting.

CHAPTER 3

PAUL

A car, a house, a monthly stipend, a job, security, a man who loved her; enough was never enough for this woman Paul thought as he attempted to shake the sharp pain from his hand before pouring the aged scotch over his bruised and swollen knuckles into a cup. Satisfied that the sting from the alcohol had cleansed his cuts and his glass was full, he threw the drink down his throat, not even bothering to wipe away the spillage from his lips.

"Do you think that you can talk to me like that and there not be any consequences? I give you everything, and threatening me is how you repay me? It's because we have history why I won't throw you out, but to keep having this conversation is getting tiring. You know why I can't leave!"

Paul had never hit her before, but she had gone too far this time. He had big plans for his future, and any slip-ups could kill all of it or leave him dead. Looking at his watch, it was 5:30 PM. Paul realized that he had only an hour to gather his thoughts for the elaborate dinner that his wife, Sandra, had planned with her parents. Usually, Paul hated entertaining his in-laws because they never knew when to leave, but for this occasion, Paul couldn't have been more ecstatic. He planned to announce his intent to resign from City Councilmen to run for Mayor. Paul had enough of the little politics and power that being on the City Council provided. He had ambitions on a bigger scale, and if Madisin was hinting at releasing even one of his secrets, he couldn't trust her to keep any of the others. Paul heard Madisin's pain-filled moan from across the room and turned just in time to watch her shocked expression go blank. As she held on to the bookshelf with one hand and pinched her blood splotched nose, with her head titled back, Paul almost began to think twice about hitting her, almost. Standing tall, Paul pretended he didn't see Madisin approaching him, nose still pinched, with a slow and steady stroll that somehow turned him on. It wasn't until he felt his shaft start to rise that he began to feel ashamed. The room seemed to close in on him, and a nervous sweat seemed to build on his neck. He felt the heat from Madisin as she slinked past him unsteadily.

Madisin making a point not to touch him didn't go unnoticed, neither did the sharp but quick glance in her eyes that told him this spat was not over yet. He read that look loud and clear. It was the look he saw his mother give his father every time she thought he embarrassed them by loud talking her in front of guests. It was the same look his wife gave him when she was ready to go to war over something he had said or did and that she did not agree. The quiet and distant demeanor that Madisin had taken on left Paul unsure of what he should do next. If she yelled and screamed or hit him back, he would be more prepared to take control of the situation. But the silent treatment was unexpected.

Paul watched Madisin as she slowly wiped the blood from her nose and then examined the damage to her face in the mirror. The silence had gone on for too long, and Paul needed to take charge of the situation before, "whack" Paul's thoughts interrupted.

Grabbing the side of his head to dull the pain, he was stopped in his tracks by an open hand slap to the left side of his head. Madisin hadn't been as hurt as he thought, and he wasn't necessarily surprised by her comeback either.

This instance would be their first big altercation involving blows, but his Maddie always had a fiery attitude.

"You are going to pay for that Paul Christen, and it's going to take more than your "love," she quoted with her fingers, "or your funky ass money to keep my mouth shut."

Paul watched Madisin as she gathered the rest of her clothes, putting them on effortlessly, and grabbed her bag on the way to the door.

Stopping in front of him, "Plenty of men would love to be with me, and instead here I am waiting on you. Someone who can't even admit to who they are. Someone to give in to their love for me, for our daughter and leave your wife."

Voice raised, Paul asked "but what about my daughter? I can't leave Sandra without considering Christina."

"Shit, you know as well as I do that you don't like that little hussy either."

"Watch your mouth!" Paul scolded. "That's no way to talk for a lady. And she's only twelve. How can she be a hussy already?"

"Well, my dirty mouth is part of the reason why we've lasted this long isn't it Mr. Christen."

Paul listened with his eyes more than his ears as Madisin said each word slowly while running her tongue across her top lip and grabbing his limp crotch, making it jump in her hand. Paul winced as Madisin squeezed him harder before quickly releasing him and making long strides toward the door again.

"You remember that OUR daughter is almost twelve too, right? I mean, you do remember that WE have a daughter?" Paul heard her emphasis on the "our" and "we" very clearly. "She's smart, beautiful, and impressionable. I mean, how long do you expect me to raise her without a father? There are plenty of men that would love to help me raise…"

Paul made it over to Madisin in the same amount of time it took her to blink and grabbed her mouth and squeezed it just tight enough for her to cut off her next few words. Breathing tense and stretching his husky frame to its full five feet eleven inches, Paul towered over Madisin. He could see the fear on her face, the way her eyes would not meet his and glanced side to side looking for an escape. Just before Paul's tight and redden lips could utter something he would regret, they were both startled by the running footsteps and sharp squeals of two little girls. Paul released Madisin just in time to catch the girls in his arms, their faces flushed from pushing the doors open to the study and both looking like Paul but in different ways.

At eleven years old, Tatiana Foster had skin the color of peanut butter with brick-colored brownish red tendrils, courtesy of Paul, that Madisin liked to brush into a curly poof at the top of her head. Her eyes were big, and almond-shaped like Madisin's and her nose was a little wide for her face, but if staring between Paul and Tatiana for too long, there would be no denying it was definitely his nose. Her long wiry legs led up to an equally long torso that would surely develop into a knockout someday if she got blessed with her mother's genes.

While Christina had the same lean frame and brighter red hair, her curls were not as tight nor as thick, so instead of ponytails, her mother Sandra, let Christina's long hair fall down her back with a few pins in the front so it wouldn't fall into her eyes. If Sandra wasn't so arrogant and self-righteous, Paul knew she would have noticed the subtle resemblance years ago. But her better than everyone else attitude kept his secrets at a safe distance.

After hugging the girls, Paul noticed his wife, Sandra leaning against the sliding door and looking at him with squinted eyes. Paul never liked to assume his wife's demeanor because she became out of sorts for all sorts of reasons, so he put the girls down and walked over to his wife and gave her a peck on the cheek. When she didn't turn away, he knew her attitude wasn't towards him this time, and for that, he was grateful. He had enough going on with one woman to have to decide how to make things up to two women. He didn't know what had gotten into Madisin lately. She wasn't usually so demanding or argumentative, but he guessed there was a first for everything.

CHAPTER 4

MADISIN

Watching Paul kiss his wife would usually make her stomach turn, but this was one of those times she could smirk because she knew what his face had to smell like. Not wanting to cause more of a scene, but knowing when to take her queue to exit, Madisin quickly cleared her throat and began to walk through the same exit that Paul and his wife were holding their latest fake love scene.

Sandra was always so extra, thinking that if she acted like everything was okay, it would be. Oh, how naïve she was. Even Madisin knew that all the pretending she did to be happy with her and Paul's arrangement was going to one day fall and if they had been any sooner coming into the room, today might have been that day. She hadn't forgotten that he had put his hands on her either. Good for him that her nose stopped bleeding and her chocolate skin that he claimed to love so much didn't bruise as easily as his. Or maybe not. Because now that she was standing on the left side of his head, she did see a strawberry colored bruise through his low cut hair, and his ear was a little swollen. She just knew that he was going to have one hell of a time explaining that later. But she could care less about that. She had her own troubles to figure out.

Grabbing her baby girl's hand and patting little Christina's head, Madisin cleared the tension from her throat again to get the two love birds to move out of the doorway which she wouldn't be surprised if Sandra were trying to block on purpose.

*

Even though she never said anything to Madisin directly, Madisin always believed that Paul's wife had been suspicious of them since the day he hired her. She made it known that there were other, more qualified candidates that he could have hired from their neighborhood. Madisin took that to plainly mean that Sandra didn't want a black woman, as fine as herself, with only an AA degree, working for her husband when there were plenty of white young men and women with four year degrees, and whose parents made sure they graduated from esteemed colleges that could serve as his Executive Assistant with no extra qualms. It didn't make the situation any better when Paul put her through two more years of college and paid for the private music and Spanish tutor for the child that Sandra only knew as Madisin's illegitimate burden among other things that she may or may not have been privy to over the last eleven years.

Sandra cut a sharp eye at Madisin.

"Excuse me, Ms. Christen. We will be on our way now. I know Babygirl has a lot of homework that she needs to get done. Y'all have a good night now." Madisin felt both the heat from Sandra's gaze and the unease from Paul's but refused to look at either. That was until Sandra grabbed her wrist and looked at the gold and diamond charm bracelet that glimmered faintly on her wrist. Madisin's eyes popped up and met Sandra's in an instant.

"That is a very nice piece you have there. I don't believe you wore this last week."

Irritated with Sandra's passive-aggressive comment and furious that she would have the audacity to touch her, Madisin took a mental breath and tried to play it cool. "Yes, it's new. It was a gift."

"From a male friend, I suppose. It looks like you may need to give Madisin here more time off Paul. Maybe then she would have enough time for one of these gifting male friends to stick and actually become a father for little Tatiana".

Madisin was used to Sandra's snide and funky ass comments, but she and her husband were treading on fragile ice today. She looked at Paul with the "you better get your bitch" stare. If Paul didn't want his wife to experience some of what he just got, he better get her situated. Looking back at Sandra, Madisin took a deep breath and pushed Tatiana further behind her with her other arm. She could feel her nosiness peeking and wanted to spare her child from this nonsense if she could.

It was Paul who should be handling this situation, but Madisin mustered up her most respectful gaze and asked, "Ma'am did you need something before I left for the day?" while gently pulling her arm back and giving Paul another warning glare.

Just as Madisin was going to let her other arm fly and let Sandra have it right across her face, Paul jumped in, "Baby," Madisin hated when he called her that in front of her, wife or not. "Let Maddie go on home. It's been a long day. I'm sure whatever is needed, we can work it out together." Paul gently took his wife's hand and slid between her and Madisin, giving his wife a peck on the lips.

As mad as Madisin was she couldn't help but to crease the side of her face with a smirk as she took their daughter's hand to leave for the home that he paid outright for her in the new shiny 2006 black Maxima that he bought her. He told Sandra that the car was the result of some employee appreciation giveaway, in which he was coerced to participate. She knew that one day soon, she would have the last laugh, and Paul would come kicking and screaming or not at all. Either way, she would have the last laugh.

CHAPTER 5

VERDELL

The wind kicked Verdell in the face as he walked out of his building. The sun was getting low. He had to hurry if he was going to make it in time to see Missy before she went to night service with her folks. After pulling his jacket collar around his neck, Verdell thrust his hands deep into his pockets to find some warmth. He crossed over the usually busy 22nd Street four-way on a mission. He had some news to tell his lady that he couldn't give her over the phone.

*

It had been close to a year since they graduated high school and he found out that he lost every single one of his scholarships to USF. The money he had saved was enough to cover his apartment and tuition for one semester. But what good was that going to be if he couldn't find a job to help him fund the rest. He had looked everywhere, but word got around fast that he was a hothead, especially since his incident with DJ made the local paper. No one would hire him for fear that his temper would quote "explode at any time" and "make him a liability" unquote. Even his own father had stopped bringing him on jobs because his customers made sure that he knew about their distaste for troublemakers and thugs on their property and asked both him and his boy to leave. With no money coming into the house, his father made it clear that nothing in this world was free, including room and board in his house. He wasn't too keen on Verdell sitting at home wasting his cool air and eating up all of his food either. Verdell's father gave him two choices. He could either enlist or get out, and he had less than 30 days to do one or the other. That one-sided conversation took place exactly twelve days ago, and his pops made sure that he knew that he only had 18 days left by putting the countdown on the fridge so he could see it every morning. His father was such an asshole.

*

"Hello Ms. Washington," Verdell absently waved and nodded in her direction, as he passed her porch. He would usually have more of a conversation with her to see if she needed him to do anything around her house, but he was in a bit of a rush today. He didn't want to ask only to be friendly either because she always had something for him to do. Whether it was going to the store, pulling the weeds out of her planters, or taking out week-old garbage, Ms. Washington didn't care what the neighbors were saying about him, she considered Verdell a blessing and made sure to tell him so. With her husband run off years ago and her sons fighting in the new war on terror, he felt a little inconsiderate walking past her the way he did, but his mind was somewhere else tonight.

Verdell had finally made up his mind about what he wanted to do and was all too aware of how his decision could change things between him and Missy. Making this move without her was not an option. Verdell loved her too much.

*

They had been together since the tenth grade, and she had stuck by his side when it seemed like the whole world turned their backs on him. It was more than evident that his father didn't want him around and Verdell sure as hell wasn't going to give his father the satisfaction of kicking him out. A lot had changed in the past eight years in his household. Ever since his mother passed, his pops had been different. Verdell didn't know if it was from sadness or guilt, but he was unquestionably colder and hardened. The things that Verdell could do to make his father happy were no longer relevant. He knew there wasn't much his father cared about these days, including him. There was a time when the lack of emotion from his father would have bothered Verdell. But now that he knew what he wanted to do with his life, to hell with his father.

Getting close to 26th and Chipco, the noise coming from around the usually quiet street corner, took Verdell out of his thoughts. It sounded like a surprise birthday party was going down in the street, and the crowd was whispering at the same time trying to get quiet for the surprise. Verdell rounded the corner and noticed that he wasn't far off with this guess. Everyone was outside crowding their porches and the streets. The sky rumbled from a loud boom, followed by what sounded like crackling fireworks. Like those around him, Verdell ducked in the middle of the brick-paved road with only his arms to cover him. He waited for the noise to stop, but when screams followed the explosions, he knew he had to get out of there. It wasn't long after rising to his feet to run back home and tell his father what was going on, that he remembered his reason for being out in this mess.

"Missy," he gasped. The commotion was coming from the direction of her parent's house. He had to check on her. Running full speed toward 26th street, Verdell slowed by the people and cars crowding the streets. It was hard to push through everyone when they were scattering in all directions to avoid a riot. He had heard about them and seen them on T.V., but to be in the middle of one did it justice. There were explosions, shattered glass, and police in every corner. The police were already here, which confirmed his suspicions that something big was going on. They never made it to his side of town fast enough to catch the action. Verdell's attempts to run through the smoke-filled and crowded street made him feel like he was running into brick walls. He would never make it through this. The smoke began burning his eyes and caused them to tear up. He knew he had to get to higher ground above the crowd and the smoke. Jumping to see over the crowd, he spotted a few street signs he was familiar with and began to plan another route. After pushing through the crowd and dodging people throwing glass bottles, rocks, and other things at the SWAT dressed police and their dogs, he finally saw Chipco Street.

There was a mob of boys around his age tipping over a charred police car. Heart racing, Verdell recognized one of those boys as Bobby Vincent. As if Bobby heard Verdell call him by name, their eyes met, and immediately Verdell knew he was looking at someone else. That boy turning over the police car was no longer the same "Dunkem" that he had played basketball with in high school. Bobby may not ever be that person again. With a simple head nod, Verdell let the warm air between them say his hello as he stayed on the opposite side of the street and continued to Missy's house.

Approaching the alley on 28th street, Verdell started counting houses, making sure that he was going to come up the back alley to the right one. He had to be very careful in this neighborhood, especially tonight.

"One…two…three…" Verdell breathlessly muttered as he passed by houses and cut through the palmettos to the mango trees that surrounded Missy's back porch.

Bam, bam, bam, bam, bam! "Missy!" Verdell screamed to

the top of his lungs. "Missy, it's me Verdell, are you okay?" Bam, bam, bam, bam, bam, he continued knocking. He didn't realize how much of a mess he must've looked until Mrs. Weiss opened the door and just stared. Her husband, Dr. Weiss, quickly arrived at the door right behind her after asking her twice who was at the door with no answer. Seeing Verdell's face, Dr. Weiss snatched Verdell into the house by his shirt collar.

"What are you doing out there boy, don't you know it's a riot going on out there? You not out there destroying what we honest black folks have worked so hard to build are you boy?"

Heaving out a heavy sigh, "no sir, Dr. Weiss." And with more excitement in his voice, "Is Missy here?"

Mrs. Weiss answered first, "YES, she is getting ready for night service. Actually, we all are getting ready to leave for service. Will you be joining us this evening?"

Looking at Mrs. Weiss' expectant face, Verdell tried to be as sincere as possible. Shaking his head no, he responded, "My father is expecting me home soon."

"As well he should," Dr. Weiss' booming voice interjected as he pulled back the kitchen blinds and sucked his teeth at the scene unfolding outside. "Nothing but the good Lord is going to save us from this." With that, Dr. Weiss left the kitchen and went into the front room gathering his hat, coat, and bible, placing his hand on Verdell's shoulder. "Missy's upstairs. Tell her she has five minutes to be downstairs or I'm coming up there to tan her hide."

Running up the stairs, Verdell shouted, "yes sir" behind him.

Making a right at the top of the stairs and walking to the last room on the left, Verdell knocked softly on the door.

"Missy," he said a lot softer this time than his first cry at her back door. When there was no answer, Verdell slowly pushed the door open. There was no sign of her in her room. "Missy" Verdell called only a little louder, and he looked behind her room door and opened her closet to peer inside. She wasn't there either.

Missy wasn't one for surprises, so Verdell felt amused that he would look in those places like they were playing some secret game of hide and seek. Walking across her room to her desk and looking out her window, made Verdell reminisce about sneaking up to see her on those late nights where he needed to let his dad sober up for a few hours before returning home. The window was still locked, and it couldn't have been locked from the outside if she indeed snuck out to see him, so she had to be upstairs somewhere. Verdell decided to take his chances and wait.

*

Turning away from the chaos outside Missy's window, Verdell glanced over her room. The walls were painted alternating stripes of pink and purple and had a few family photos of her, her two older brothers, and her parents on them. And what space wasn't taken up by a family photo was either a Prince poster or a Prince Album cover. He had promised Missy that he would take her down to the Mansion in Miami for the Tamar

Tour in a few weeks. He couldn't wait to see the look on her face when he showed her the tickets. Verdell personally likes Michael over Prince, but he would do just about anything to see a smile on her face.

*

Looking around her room, Verdell spotted a new picture. It was Missy's graduation photo. It was the biggest one surrounded by smaller pictures of Missy with friends and family on her wall behind her bed. Verdell walked closer to her bed to get a better look at the portrait. Her smooth, toffee-colored skin and slanted brown eyes were perfect. Verdell personally thought she could have given a better smile, but the smirk on the photo was more in line with her personality.

The room door opened, catching him off guard. Verdell was practically kneeling in Missy's bed trying to get a better look at the photo. Lord forbid it was Mrs. Weiss, or even worse, Dr. Weiss. That's all he needed was them seeing how comfortable he was in Missy's bed. Quickly getting out of the bed and ready to explain what he was doing, Verdell was face to face with Missy's swollen red eyes. It looked like she had been crying.

He noticed something drop to the floor but figured he must have scared her as bad as she did him and finding out the reason for why she would be crying was most important, so he disregarded. Rushing over to hug her, Verdell was surprised as Missy's sobs into his shirt came as soon as he touched her. Verdell gently pushed her away from his shirt and held her out at arm's length so he could take another look at her and make sure there wasn't anything that he missed that would alert him to there being something wrong.

Cautiously, Verdell started, "Baby, I'm glad to see you too. I didn't think it had been that long since we last saw each other. What's wrong?"

Instead of answering, Missy dropped down to the floor and tried to pick up what she dropped earlier when she walked into her room.

Verdell asked again, "Baby what's wrong? Why are you crying?" When their eyes met, Verdell saw what he thought was fear.

"Where are my parents?" Missy whispered.

"They're downstairs waiting for you to get ready so y'all can go to service, why what's up?" Verdell's voice matched her whisper.

Missy quickly shut the door behind her and took his hand and lead Verdell to her bed.

"Missy, baby, we don't have time for that. Your parents are downstairs, and I know your dad will be up here any minute because he told me to tell you that he was going to"…, pausing to make sure that he gave the phrase the right amount of sarcasm, "tan your hide if you weren't downstairs in five minutes." Verdell laughed waiting for Missy to respond and tell him to get off clowning her dad like she usually did when he made fun of him, but she still hadn't looked him in his eyes yet. Concerned, Verdell grabbed Missy's chin and turned her face to him. "Missy, baby, I came to tell you something important, and we only have a little bit of time, but I need your full attention. You have to tell me what's wrong. Did somebody hurt you?"

Missy shook her head no.

"Then talk to me." She placed something in his other hand, and Verdell looked down at it and then back up at her in shock.

"You're pregnant?" Verdell questioned.

Missy finally met his eyes for the first time since seeing him in her room and answered with a simple, "Yes."

Jumping up from the bed, Verdell asked, "well, what are you crying for?" Verdell thought that question must have been a stupid one to her because she sucked her teeth, cocked her head to the side, and folded her arms across her chest as if he should have already had the answer. But just the opposite, Verdell thought this was perfect. He picked her up and started spinning Missy in the air. Verdell began to slow as he felt Missy push against his chest. Maybe she was becoming sick or something, he thought. He heard somewhere that babies make you sick, so her being uncomfortable wouldn't come as a surprise.

"Put me down Verdell, I'm going to be sick," Missy said, confirming his thought as he placed her on her feet. "How can you laugh and be happy at something like this? You done lost your mind? My parents are going to kill me. They are going to kill you! And did you forget that I'm in school? Becoming a doctor is not easy and ain't no baby going to make that easier." Sucking her teeth again, Missy walked away from him while running her hands through her short curly hair in frustration.

"Well, how about a husband?" Verdell asked.

At hearing his words, Missy turned around faster than she could steady herself to see Verdell bent on one knee with his mother's wedding band held out to her.

"Verdell, what is this? Stop playing with me boy and get up from down there before my daddy sees you."

"Now you know I didn't give a damn about your daddy before the baby, why would I give one about him now when you carrying my baby?"

"Verdell, how many times do I have to tell you to stop disrespecting my daddy?" She slapped his shoulder and whined. Her slap stung, but determined, Verdell shrugged it off.

"All I'm saying is that your father doesn't scare me. And if he'll let me, well if you'll let me, I'll take care of you and my baby and y'all not going to want for nothing." Verdell could see the tears peeking at the corners of Missy's eyes.

"And just how are you going to do that Verdell? Huh? You don't have a job!" she said exasperated.

"See that's where you wrong," Verdell said with pride, "I did some research on enlisting and went to see a Marine recruiter who told me he could get me and my wife housing and that I could get an education and learn a trade just for serving two years." Verdell waited a minute to gauge Missy's reaction before continuing. "He also said that we would be traveling the world to somewhere new every six months. And I remember how you said you wanted to travel baby. Just say yes, and we can make this happen. We can get married tomorrow and be on a plane to our new home to get settled before I go to boot camp. You and the baby would get the best care and have everything y'all need." Verdell pleaded and looked in her puffy eyes with earnest, "What do you say, baby? Let me make this happen for us."

Missy's hesitancy was making him nervous. They had talked about marriage before, and Missy always sounded as if whenever Verdell asked, she would say yes. So why was it taking her so long to say something, anything now? Verdell was still bent on one knee when Missy stuttered in her step before walking over to him, taking his hand and attempting to pull him up from the floor.

"But what about my parents?" she asked slowly.

"What about them? They can come to the wedding. I mean we will need witnesses, baby."

Missy looked Verdell in his eyes and kissed him softly on his lips. Verdell's body tingled all over, and he started to remember how they got in her present situation in the first place. Hearing Missy's father call her name, from what seemed like the bottom of the stairs, Verdell jumped back.

"Missy! You better be ready. Tell that boy goodnight. We got to go. The police are going to be blocking off the roads soon, and I want to make it to church before they do," Dr. Weiss screamed.

Verdell surprised Missy and kissed her passionately to remind her how much he loved her.

"Baby you got to tell me something because I'm leaving here

with or without you. Especially now that you are having my baby, I'm no good to you the way I am. You deserve better, and I have to go away to be that."

Missy's large brown eyes stared into his, "Will I be able to finish school?"

Verdell kissed her again, "The very best schools," Verdell assured her.

"Okay, I'll do it." she said. "I'll marry you, Verdell."

"OOOOOweeee," he screamed as he kissed her and spun her around the room again.

Their moment was lost when both he and Missy jumped at the sound of footsteps on the stairs. Reality hit.

Whispering, Verdell told Missy, "Finish getting ready and I'll go downstairs and prep your parents on our decision." winking and stressing the OUR.

Missy excitedly went to her dresser to start fixing her face but ran back to Verdell as if she forgot something and kissed him fervently.

"I'll need my ring if I'm going to be a married woman." Missy giggled and took the now sweaty ring out of Verdell's palm and slipped it on her ring finger. It was a perfect fit.

Verdell kissed Missy again and slapped her on her butt. He watched as she hurried away with all of the joy in the world in her eyes. Verdell turned to the door, both happy and scared to share the news with the good Dr. and Mrs. Weiss.

Before he could turn the doorknob to tell Missy I love you, a loud noise exploded and threw his body into the frame of the door, making him bump his head on the wood siding.

Vision blurry, ears ringing, Verdell tried to move and focus on Missy who must have heard and felt the explosion too. Gathering himself to his feet and touching his palm to the blistering spot at the side of his head, Verdell was able to spot Missy through the dust.

"Missy?" Verdell was surprised to see Missy standing, considering the window that her dresser was in front of was broken with flames eating away at what remained of the frame. "Missy? Baby, get away from the window." Staggering to walk on shaky legs through the smoke towards Missy's still shadow, Verdell began to worry. Not only was Missy not responding, but something wasn't right.

Everything was moving in slow motion, and it seemed like he couldn't move fast enough to her even though he had to have been no more than ten steps away. When Verdell finally made it to Missy, he rounded her trembling body to see her face. The dull and hollow look, her eyes pierced him with made his stomach lurch. Determined to wake her from her shock, Verdell grabbed Missy by the shoulders and shook her.

"Missy? Missy? Baby?" Missy's eyes rolled to the back of her head before she collapsed in his arms. At the same time, Dr. Weiss burst through the door. Panicked and still rocking Missy, now slumped in his arms, to wake her, Verdell's heart broke into a million pieces as he got a good look at his soon to be wife, and the mother of his child. It was like he was seeing her face for the first time.

The blast had charred it, and she was bleeding from her eyes, ears, and nose. There were pieces of glass lodged in her face and on her hands. Verdell slowly began to pull the glass out of her face, careful not to hurt her further, and oblivious to Dr. Weiss' presence until he was right upon them.

Missy's father ran over to them and pulled Missy out of Verdell's arms shouting, "What have you done? What have you done?" The room seemed to open up, and the sound returned to Verdell's ears when he heard the rushed footsteps and screams of Mrs. Weiss.

Sitting in the dust in the burnt ruins of everything around him, Verdell's hands covered his eyes and then his ears to cover the sound of his disbelief and sorrowed moans. His mind flashed to their first kiss, the first time they laughed together, the first time she helped him through his father's disappointment, the first time they made love, his proposal, the light her face gave when she said yes, the baby.

"Oh, shit! My baby!" Looking around him, Verdell noticed that he was the only one in the room. He had to find Dr. Weiss to let them know that Missy was pregnant. He had to find out if Missy was okay. It never occurred to him that Missy's father was a doctor who could've helped her when he first entered the room.

Now that the shock had worn off, "She's pregnant" Verdell shouted over and over as he ran down the first set of stairs and then jumped down the second and through the front door where he found reality. Verdell's shirt and hands had Missy's blood all over them.

Before he could spot Missy or her parents in the commotion, three officers ran towards him with their guns drawn and grabbed him, shouting for him to stop resisting. Verdell couldn't believe what was happening. It was too much to take in. His girlfriend; his fiancé; the love of his life; and the mother of his child were clinging to life, and he was getting arrested. For what? Verdell frantically searched the front yard for Missy and Dr. Weiss and Mrs. Weiss to help him. They would be able to clear up this misunderstanding.

Not seeing them, "This must be some misunderstanding," Verdell said, hoping that the cops would release him or at least loosen their grip to listen and help him make sense of this mess.

He didn't realize how wrong he was until he felt a sharp smack on his back. Struck again on his shoulder and hearing more metal slide and click before being struck on both his legs, Verdell stopped moving in hopes that the pain gathering throughout his body and rushing to his chest would stop. Grunting while struggling to shift his weight to his feet, Verdell's body was drug to the police car waiting at the curb. At his wit's end, Verdell started screaming for help but quieted when he saw Dr. Weiss and his wife with what appeared to be Missy on a gurney by an ambulance on the street.

Verdell screamed at anyone who would lend him a sympathetic ear and get him out of these cuffs, "I'm her fiancé. Check her hand. We got engaged tonight, and she is pregnant with my baby. I love her. Dr. Weiss, I love your daughter."

The cuffs tightened on Verdell's wrists, and the officers

quickened their pace to the cruiser. Dr. Weiss wouldn't even look at him.

"At least tell me how she is?" Verdell yelled. "How is she, how is our baby?" They continued to ignore him, which just made Verdell struggle harder to get a closer look for himself.

Verdell's head banged against the top of the opened police door, and his vision started to spin and blur. Drained both mentally and physically, Verdell mashed his face on the window to try and stop his head from throbbing, and to catch a glance of Missy, but all he heard and saw were the sirens as they drove into the night.

CHAPTER 6

DHORIAN

"Uggggh Pop" Dhorian Jr. groaned and pulled his pillow over his head. "I told you, I didn't want to be no damn undertaker." At 19, DJ still hadn't figured out what he wanted to do with his life.

*

His father was the only Mortician in the Bay area that provided burials for every budget and had been in business as long as Dhorian could remember. Their line of work was never short, and he always needed a hand. His father had taught him everything there was to know about the company. He had even openly expressed the desire to keep the business in the family. But Dhorian was not having it. After that dumb ass fight with his cousin, his basketball scholarships to Michigan, Miami, and USF were all revoked due to disorderly conduct on the court. Who would've thought a few challenging words would jeopardize his entire future and the only plan he had to get out of the Bay? He did all right in school, but most of his smarts came from common sense and the streets. There was no test he couldn't pass with a little last-minute studying. If that didn't work, Dhorian was able to talk himself into or out of any grade he deemed necessary. He was just that good. But none of the subjects ever really stuck with him. Basketball was the only real reason he kept up with his grades anyway. His father tried to talk him into finding his calling by going to a HBCU. But Dhorian didn't see the point in spending money he didn't have to be taught how to make the kind of money their education couldn't guarantee him. It was that simple. He needed big money for the rich and famous lifestyle he always imagined for himself and college wasn't going to get him that. Dhorian thought of other ways to fund his dreams past his basketball career, but he couldn't think of anything that wouldn't take forever, end up with him being in jail, or dead. And Dhorian wasn't going out like that. So, for the past six months, he had been sulking watching reruns of "Diff'rent Strokes" and "Night Court" and the new season of "Law and Order." He was really getting into that one. Being a lawyer had to be better than removing organs, pumping formaldehyde, and painting over bug holes. And anything had to be better than that smell.

*

"Boy, who you taking that tone with? Get your ass up out of that bed 'for I whip it up out of there."

Dhorian continued shuffling angrily through his sheets and made his way out of bed. He almost jumped out of his skin when his father met him halfway and yanked him the rest of the way out and onto his feet. Dhorian felt a close to unbearable chill when his bare feet hit the cold wood floor. He was definitely up now, and he couldn't seem to keep still.

"Stop all that bouncing, boy. Now listen to me."

Dhorian felt his brain rattle as his father shook his shoulders. It was way too early in the morning for this. Looking up into his father's eyes though made him straighten up quick. Early morning or not, Dhorian knew being yanked from bed would be the least of his worries if his father had to repeat himself. He never had reason to be afraid of his father, but Dhorian knew when he meant business, and this was one of those times.

"Ok, pop, I'm up, and I'm listening. What's up?"

"What's up boy, is that I'm sending you on an internship with Mr. Paul Christen."

Dhorian's face instantly brightened despite the gritty eye boogers he had weighing down the corners of his eyelids. Everybody knew who Paul Christen was. He was a business mogul turned councilman and had a commercial on television saying that he was running for Mayor. Dhorian didn't know all of the details, but Mr. Paul Christen made that cash. Which means if he got with him, he could make that cash too.

"Seriously! Pops don't play me."

"Boy, your mother would be so disappointed in your mouth, God bless her soul."

Just his father's mention of his mother dampened his excitement. Dhorian shifted his gaze to the ground trying to avert his father's eyes, trying to hide the tightness in his throat, the burning that pulled at his neck and nostrils. He didn't do it quick enough for his father not to notice the change in his mood, however fortunately for him, his father quickly changed the subject back to business matters.

"I ran into Mr. Christen's wife at the fresh fruit market the other day, and she casually mentioned that her husband was having a hard time winning the votes of the people in our district."

Interrupting, Dhorian asked, "You mean black votes, Pop?"

"MMM-hmmm, Mr. Smart-ass," his father mumbled and passed him the side-eye before he continued slowly. "Well, like I was saying, she said he was having a hard time winning the votes of the black folk and mentioned that they were looking for ways to gain our support."

It didn't come as a surprise to Dhorian that his father was privy to this type of information. He had an outstanding reputation for being very thorough in his line of work. Along the way, Dhorian's father had made some reputable and influential friends that came with all types of requests for special services. Those weren't usually offered in the brochure or to the public. Dhorian Sr. had a way of hearing his clients between the lines, and Dhorian watched his father all these years acquiring some of those skills too. His father was a trusted member of the community, and if he could get Mr. Christen to trust him as well, there was no telling how close he could be to his dream.

Dhorian watched his father cross his room to his closet, waiting for him to finish. His father had his full attention. This opportunity might be the break he was finally waiting for. When Dhorian Sr. turned and looked at his son with a coal grey suit and silk burgundy tie in his hands, Dhorian's face immediately scrunched into a grimace as he sank back onto the bed.

He hadn't worn a getup like that since his mother passed and had refused to wear one ever since. Somehow though, the suits continued to miraculously appear in his closet. Dhorian ran his hands down the front of his face trying to keep the memories at bay, but like the rest of his life, he couldn't get control, and they resurfaced anyway.

*

Sitting in the front pew of the small Missionary Baptist Church, arms folded tight across a chest that was on fire from heartache, Dhorian's body was numb. Even though his chest and throat were tight, he wrestled with his tears and refused to let them fall.

There were people Dhorian had never seen crying louder than he and his father, and they were doing enough crying and shouting for everyone. His face was hot with anger as the choir sang, "I feel like going on." How in the hell could they know what she wanted? She didn't want to go anywhere. She wouldn't have gone anywhere without him. His father refused to let anyone else prepare her and made him suffer through helping. Thankfully his father only had him dress his mother and help him place her in the Tiffany blue satin-lined casket that Dhorian had picked out for her. His father told him that helping to prepare his mother for the next life would help him get through the pain of losing her in this one. But getting over suicide was his issue, not losing his mother. Everyone has to go at some time. It was a hard but real lesson that he learned young working with his father, but to lose his mother....

*

"DJ, did you hear me, boy?"

Snapping back from the memories, Dhorian surprised himself when he answered his father a little louder than he wanted.

"I'll do it!"

His father was giving him what he'd grown to know as the stare of discernment. Clearing his throat and squaring his shoulders to face his father before answering again.

"I'll do it, Pops."

There was an eternity of silence that passed under his father's intense gaze before he finally heard him say, "Good. The interview is in a week. We don't have long to get you ready."

CHAPTER 7

MADISIN

Madisin's eyes fluttered as the sun's rays played with the wind and cast shadows over her face through the lace in her curtains. Stretching the full length of her queen mattress, Madisin dreaded the thought of remembering what day it was. Her head hurt, her body ached, and her face felt swollen around her eyes from all the crying she had done these past few days. She couldn't remember a time in her life where she had cried as hard. Pulling herself out of bed, Madisin dragged her worn body to the bathroom to see if she looked as bad as she felt. The bright light from the small vanity made her squint as she touched the bruise on her face. She was so busy trying to focus her eyes on the damage that she almost missed her Babygirl's handwriting on the Strawberry Shortcake notebook paper taped to the wall next to the mirror. She had bought her Babygirl the small notebook last Christmas because she said she wanted to be a reporter like that Fox 13 anchorwoman Denise White.

"Nana said we should let you sleep because you weren't feeling well. But don't worry because she made me hot links and eggs and said she would walk me to school. If you feel better later, could you come pick me up? Hope you feel better. Love your Babygirl. P.S. – Nana said she sure hopes you're not expecting. Expecting what momma? Okay got to go, see you soon."

Madisin winced as she smiled through the pain that shot through her cheek. She would have to remember to thank Mama later for filling in for her. After a hot shower and an extra-strong cup of coffee, Madisin sat at the kitchen table deep in thought over last Friday's turn of events. She still couldn't believe that Paul hit her. And not only did Paul hit her, but his arrogant ass didn't apologize for it either.

*

If she only remembered bits and pieces of what happened, that was the chunk of memory that hurt her more than her busted nose. Paul had never even spoken to her in anger before that instance. Everything since Friday had been in slow motion and Madisin had the entire weekend to think about and replay the madness from the life-size movie reel. In light of the craziness that recently overtook her life, Madisin decided to play hooky today. The last thing she wanted to do was see Paul after their previous argument. He had another thing coming if he thought she was just going to sit and wait another twelve years for him to come to his senses. As Madisin rose up from the kitchen table, she knew first things first. She needed to throw away all the un-meaningful shit he ever gave her. After that, she would then deep scrub him off her body.

*

Madisin was waiting at the gated entrance right at 2:30 PM when Babygirl got out of school. Her daughter ran into her arms and gave her a tight hug. At the age of eleven, Madisin couldn't believe that her daughter was almost as tall as her. Squeezing her daughter tight, she prayed that no matter how big she would get, her baby girl would always know that her mother would be here to hug her just like she was now.

"Want to go get some ice cream?" Madisin asked her only child. Squealing with joy and showing her snaggle-teeth Babygirl smiled back up at her.

"Oooo momma, can we get Nana some too and take it home to her?"

"Sure thing baby girl." Tatiana Foster, who Madisin affectionately referred to as Babygirl, had a huge grin on her face. Babygirl's smile was just the type of distraction Madisin needed to keep her mind off Paul.

*

Even though Paul paid her very well to keep his books and file paperwork, he paid her, even more, when they got into their spats. His guilt always leads him to compensate her for putting up with his shit. And it didn't fail today either. No later had she gotten out of the shower, there was a white-glove service delivery from Paul with a single yellow rose, which he knew was her favorite color, an I'm sorry note, and $5,000. Which was almost three times what he would normally send. Besides being married and an occasional asshole, he wasn't all that bad. He took excellent care of them. She nor Babygirl had any wants. Everything they needed; Paul made sure they had before she could even ask. This luxury didn't make her live extravagantly or outside of her means. No one would ever know by looking at her that she was secretly a quarter millionaire. Not even her mother or her Babygirl knew, and that was saying a lot because nothing went unnoticed by her beautiful Babygirl, who happened to be eleven and hated to be called Babygirl.

*

Stopping in her tracks and making a strange face, Babygirl looked into Madisin's eyes.

"Mommy, but it's not the 15th."

"What do you mean, baby?" Eyebrows furrowed, Madisin noticed the serious look on her Babygirl's face.

"I mean it's not payday, right? We don't have money for ice-cream today?"

Even though Madisin was great at saving money, so they had plenty, she wanted to teach her Babygirl to be reasonable with her money and not spend just because it was burning holes in her pockets. Kneeling and looking up into her child's sad eyes, "Yes I know baby, but Mr. Christen gave me a little extra today, and it's okay if we do something nice just this one time. You still want that ice cream, don't you?"

"Yes, ma'am." Babygirl said smirking through her pout. Her mood changed, Madisin couldn't help but giggle with her daughter as she was dragged and made to skip the next five blocks to Bo's ice-cream shop.

Madisin ordered a Strawberry-banana shake. The one with the real strawberries and bananas. Babygirl ordered a sundae in a cone with a bowl for safety, and they ordered Nana a pint of Butter Pecan that they would stop back to the window to pick up when they were done eating theirs and were ready to go home. Babygirl's idea. As they sat down at one of the empty stone benches and table, the warm sun beamed on their faces, and they began to people watch as their minds took them into the lives of the people passing by. After several minutes of silence and to Madisin's surprise, she heard sniffling. Startled, she looked up from her shake and over at her daughter.

"Babygirl are you crying? What's wrong?" Madisin immediately found a napkin, spit in it and started to rub at her child's cheeks.

Pulling away and whining, "Maaaa, you know I hate it when you call me Babygirl."

"Well, what do you expect when I hear my Babygirl crying? What's wrong honey?" Madisin said as she used her napkin to wipe the tears from the sides of her face, still trying to get her daughter to look at her. "Honey? Tatiana? Look at mommy, what's wrong?"

Tatiana finally looked at her mother and accidentally pushed her half-eaten sundae cone to the ground and started bawling in her mother's shirt. Some of the people walking by started to stare and Madisin couldn't stand nosey people. She had to get this girl together and then they could talk about what was bothering her so. Madisin took her Babygirl by her shoulders and shook her just enough to get her attention.

"Now listen to me, Tatiana. I don't know what's bothering you, but mommy can't help you through your tears. They are going to fall all on their own. I need you to talk to me. Now wipe those tears and fix your face." Madisin said as she handed her daughter some napkins and scooted back from her daughter's side of the table to give her some breathing room and to let the outside air cool her face.

"I'm sorry momma," Tatiana sniffed.

"No need to be sorry baby. You were just so happy a few minutes ago. I can't imagine what it could have been to make you so sad, so quick. Is it school? Somebody messing with you? Is it boys? Cause if its boys, let me tell you one damn thing." Madisin felt herself getting worked up, but before she could finish, she felt her daughter's small hand grab her chin and turn her head to a small park across the street. There was a man and a woman playing what looked like hide and seek with their two young children through the swings and monkey bars. Madisin immediately dropped her head and kissed her daughter's hand. Tatiana didn't have questions about her father often, but Madisin knew this would be one of those times. She sighed and looked at her baby.

"I guess it is getting late, huh, baby?" Tatiana looked in the trees like she knew the time by the sun's shadow and nodded so hard the ponytails in her head danced. "Come on, baby. Let's go home." Madisin kissed her Babygirl's forehead, took her hand while throwing away their unfinished shakes and sundaes in the garbage, and they began walking home.

Even though they didn't have long before they reached their steps, Madisin wanted to try to explain the daddy situation to Tatiana without getting too sensitive. She couldn't stand to see her Babygirl crying. Her big doe brown eyes, her wide nose, and her burnt orange hair reminded her so much of her father. Anything she could do to cheer her Babygirl up she would try to do.

"Let me tell you a story." Madisin watched Tatiana's face perk up instantly.

"Ooooo mommy, I love stories."

"I know you love stories," she said while tickling her neck. As Madisin started her story, she opened the screen door to their front porch. Sitting down on the steps, Madisin began, "One summer, not such a long time ago there was a little girl who moved with her family into a new neighborhood. She was a little nervous because she didn't have any friends where they were moving to, but she was in luck. Next door there was a friend just waiting to play with her. And they played all summer. They friends watched the stars, they went camping, they ate dinner at each other's houses, and they skipped rocks"

"Wait! Mommy that doesn't sound like playing to me. Where's the Xbox 360 or the movies or the Chuck E Cheese?"

"Well that just means that you are spoiled, and I did say once upon a time right, besides whose telling the story, me or you"

Tatiana giggled "You!"

"Okay well let me finish. So after the summer finished, it was time for them to start school, and they were so excited that they would be going to the same school. But that happiness was short-lived. The little girl's friend got picked on at the school because of the way he looked. He didn't look like the rest of the kids that went to the school, and it got so bad that he stopped coming to school. The little girl would run home after school looking for her friend, and he would look out of the window refusing to come out and refusing to play with the little girl. She was heartbroken. He went away."

"That's a very sad story, mommy."

"But no, baby. After some time they found each other again and fell madly in love. They were together all the time, but something was different about her friend, he wasn't the same nice little boy she knew all those years ago. It was like he didn't like himself because of getting teased all those years before, and he pretended for everyone else."

"Well, what was different about him momma?"

"He looked, different baby. He didn't have brown or dark-colored skin like me and you. He had pale skin like …"

"Like a white man!" Tatiana finished with shock.

"Yes he did," Madisin confirmed.

"Well that's easy momma, it's nothing wrong with being white."

"But that's just it baby, he wasn't white, he was black like us. His skin was just different. He had red hair…"

"Oooo ooo like mine!" Tatiana shouted.

"Yes, baby just like yours but brighter" Madisin smiled slowly and fingered her Babygirl's hair.

"Okay, so what happened?" Tatiana asked eagerly.

"Even though she could see something was going on with him, she still decided to love him because he never treated her any different. And their love grew, it grew so much that they had a beautiful baby girl. She was so beautiful. She was a perfect mix of both of them. And he loved that Babygirl something awful." And then solemnly, Madisin said "but then it was time for him to leave again. The man told his friend, who he loved and had a beautiful newborn baby with, that he already had a family and he had to be there with them because it's where he belonged, where he fit in. No matter how hard she pleaded, she couldn't get him to stay. Her heart left broken again."

"Oh no momma, did she ever see him again? What happened to the baby?"

"She saw him around now and then, and when they would see each other, he would love on his baby sooo much, but they would never be together again as a family." As Madisin finished the story, she pushed Tatiana's curly red hair back from her eyes and lifted her face to hers. "Moral of the story baby girl is that sometimes it's easier to focus on other people's pain than your own. You understand?"

Tatiana shrugged her shoulders, "I guess momma, but next time I'm telling the story. Yours are getting weird."

Madisin laughed and hugged her Babygirl.

Then Tatiana pulled back abruptly, "Momma? Yes, baby? You weren't trying to tell me that we are white, were you?"

Madisin laughed so hard that her stomach hurt and said, "no baby" as they both stood up. She patted Tatiana on the bottom and told her to take the ice cream in the house and wash up for dinner before Nana had a fit about the melted ice cream in the fridge.

"Yes, ma'am." Tatiana ran in the house just quick enough not to witness the tears that began to stream down her mother's face.

Madisin hurt for her friend, for her love, and her Babygirl.

"Come on in here, baby." Madisin heard a stern, but soothing voice say. She turned around and in the old wooden doorway stood her mother. Madisin rose quickly from the stairs, ran into her arms, and buried her face into her mother's apron, not the least turned away by the flour, or what she thought was flour. "Them tears are going to fall all on their own baby. Come on in and eat and we can talk after Babygirl goes off to bed. Now fix your face and get in here. It's getting cold."

Madisin laughed through her fading tears and said, "Yes ma'am" as they closed the door behind them.

CHAPTER 8

VERDELL

"Please say your name after the beep," the female voice said.

"Yo Pop, it's me, Verdell, I'm in trou." before he could finish his line connected and his father's weary voice answered the phone. "Hello? Hello?" "Yo Pop, it's me. I'm in trouble, and I need you to come get me."

After clearing his throat loudly, his father answered, "Come get you? Come get you from where?"

"Pop I'm, I'm."

His father cut him off. "Yea, yea. I know where you are. I heard that lady say it was Orient Road Jail when I picked up the phone."

Relieved that his dad was starting to get the picture, Verdell asked. "Okay Pops so when can you come get me?"

"Come get you?" His father hesitated. "Well, they had to put you in there for a reason. What did you do?"

Explaining things was taking longer than Verdell thought it would, and seeing the other inmates and the officer getting antsy around him made him nervous. He just wanted to be out of here.

"Dad listen. I don't have much time. They say I killed or, or tried to kill Missy, but, but I didn't Pop. I swear. I love her. We are getting married. She's pregnant with my baby. With your grandchild Pops. I have to get out to check on her." Verdell listened to the dead air on the phone, waiting for his father to break the silence.

"Get off the phone!" he heard someone yell from behind him.

Trying not to show his fear, Verdell grabbed the phone tight and pressed it closer to his face. "Pop, you still there?"

Sighing heavily again before responding, he thought he heard his Pops say "Ain't nothing I can do for you son."

Ears ringing from all the noise around him and straining to hear or understand his father's words, Verdell pressed his face as far into the phone as possible and said, "Pops repeat that. I… I almost got to go." Verdell placed his finger in his open ear to make the line clearer. "You heard me say I didn't do it right?"

His father cleared his throat, and his voice came through loud and clear. "Yea, I heard you Verdie."

Verdell hadn't heard his father call him Verdie since before his mother died.

"But it looks like you've dug yourself into a hole that only the Good Lord can get you out of. Call me in a few days to let me know what's going on."

Verdell was too hurt to continue the conversation, but he was more afraid of what hanging up the phone and accepting his fate meant. So he decided to make one last plea. He was trying not to sniffle and avoid sound as tight as his throat felt. "Pop. I'm telling you…I didn't do it. I can't stay in here Pop." Now speaking through the hot tears that were sliding freely into his mouth, "please don't leave me in here."

Just as the line went dead, he heard the guard yell his way, "inmate times up on the phone. If no one's coming for you, proceed toward the yellow door walking inside those arrows for processing!"

After being stripped naked, bent over, told to squat, and pushed into a small, grimy, and cold cell with someone he didn't know, Verdell just wanted to go to sleep and never wake up. He didn't speak and barely ate over the next two days. His cellmate, a young Spanish guy about his age, tried to make small talk, but Verdell made it clear that he was uninterested. By the time Monday came, he couldn't even remember using the bathroom. The first night he woke up in a cold sweat after a dream where he saw Missy holding a bloody baby, his baby, in her arms and she had a burning hole right through her stomach. The images had Verdell so upset that he vomited. Head fully emerged in the already disgusting toilet bowl. It wasn't until his stomach stopped heaving and he pulled up that he realized that there was something other than the insides of his stomach in that bowl.

Verdell's guilt about Missy and the baby gave him a sickening feeling in the pit of his stomach. His fear of being in jail made his head swirl. For the first couple of days, he tried to convince himself that Missy wasn't dead. He never saw her body. He just knew she was hurt, not dead. And not because of him. He slunk back to his bed to curl back into his assumed position.

The following Monday morning, Verdell woke up to hard taps on the bars and his last name like he was miles away. He didn't know how long the guard called his name when he finally stirred and faced the guard. But by the crease lines around his reddening forehead and mouth, he knew it had to be for a while because the guard looked pretty agitated. Not wanting to end up like the actual criminals he saw on those Scared Straight documentaries by irritating the guard even further, Verdell quickly stood up and slowly approached the iron bars. He felt so weak that he had to work hard at not falling on his way over to the guard, which couldn't have been more than the usual steps.

"Yes, sir?"

"Next time yo ass move slow as molasses when I call your name, I'm going to make sure to put something on yo ass that will make you move faster than the Daytona 500."

Verdell stared at the guard and then looked at his bunkmate, who quickly turned away, not sure what to say or how serious to take the threat.

"You hear me, boy?"

"Yes, sir," Verdell said a little louder than he had intended.

"Good! Now, you got a visitor. Give me your wrists and follow me."

Verdell stuck his wrists through the slotted square opening between the bars where the guard met him with iron cuffs and snapped them roughly around his wrists. Wincing at the pain, Verdell looked at the guard ready to say something slick but thought twice about it when the guard's tomato colored and ever creasing face dared him to do so.

The public defender that Verdell met with looked like he couldn't have been much older than he was. His suit was a plain polyester and a size too big. The courtroom felt like a small wooden box and smelled like sweat and nervous energy. It was almost a relief from the shit and piss that he had been surrounded by for the last week and a half. Verdell was sure once he called his dad to explain he would be there to get him. But he hadn't heard from his father since he told him what happened. Looking around the room, Verdell attempted to identify people that he might have known, but he didn't see Missy's parents anywhere. He gave up days ago on his father showing up for him, and he knew that now since it had been confirmed that Missy was gone, thanks to his bunkmate and a news clipping with his face and the dead one of the love of his life on there, he was truly alone. Verdell tried to remain hopeful while he sat and waited for his docket, but once he saw all of the friendly eye contact that his public defender was giving the police officer, a chubby older gray-haired white guy whose face he slightly remembered from a photo in Missy's room and assumed to be her big hotshot attorney grandfather, and the Prosecutor, he knew he was going to get screwed royally by the Good Ol' Boys. Verdell forced himself to forget his arraignment. It wasn't any surprise to him that he did not have a bond.

CHAPTER 9

PAUL

Paul Christen arrived home six minutes after 9:30 PM to a house that felt more like Rikers than a home. His home. All of the grand architecture, the opulent Doric columns, the grand winding marble staircase leading into the foyer, the vast array of classical and contemporary art on every wall couldn't have made him hate the house any more than he did already. Ten thousand square feet of grandeur and all he felt was loneliness. Even with his wife, daughter, and mother in law present in the house on most occasions; the space didn't feel the same without Madisin in his life.

"Paul? Is that you?"

Paul groaned at his wife Sandra shouting down the stairs like she was sitting at the top just waiting for him to walk in the door. The sound of her voice made his throat dry. Silently, he began to pray that she didn't come down those damn stairs.

Before he could answer, Sandra started nagging, which had become the norm as of late.

"Paul, are you just getting home? You said you would be home by 7:30 PM to spend some time and eat dinner with your family. Mother and I waited as long as we could for you and Christina, your daughter, was practically starving and you didn't even have the decency to call and let us know you would be late. As much as I do for you and this family, you'd think someone in your position would show more gratitude to have a wife that cares as much as I do. You can be so selfish sometimes."

Paul rubbed the tension from his temples and tried to control his breathing. He found himself short of breath lately. Especially when in stressful situations like now. Maddie had gotten him some meditation music a few months ago to help him with what she thought could have been high blood pressure. But he shook it off. The mediation music did teach him some mantras and breathing techniques that he found useful, especially in situations like now. Paul inhaled a sharp slow breath filling his lungs, and then exhaled in three short bursts. He repeated this three times before walking further into the foyer and making his way to the kitchen. When he saw Sandra making her way down the stairs, he groaned as his chest tightened.

Watching her pink chiffon robe dance in the space around her as she trotted down the stairs in all her self-righteousness, Paul chuckled at how she exaggerated the facts of his absence. His child would never starve. But the thought only made him think of Madisin and their daughter. Would they go hungry without him? His wife had finally made it to where he was shifting through the day's mail in the sitting room outside his home office. Her lavender perfume greeted him before she did. Breathing in the scent, Paul remembered a time where he used to love his wife's smell, her pouty lips, and big begging eyes. Now, the odor only reminded him of how needy she was, and how much he needed to be anywhere else but here. Sandra always needed something from him. She never once asked him about his day or how he was feeling or cared about all that he went through to keep up the lifestyle that they had grown accustomed. It was always about Sandra. But, his Madisin took care of him; she was the exact opposite. Could he even think of her as "his" Madisin anymore? Their arguments were never as intense as this last one, and she always came back. But what she knows, the information she threatened him with, it could oust him, could ruin everything, all of his hard work. He would have to think about what to do about that at a later time. Now, he was exhausted.

Instead of replying to what he felt like was another of Sandra's rhetorical monologues, Paul decided to play up the sorry husband bit and kissed Sandra gently on her temple and said in the most loving and understanding tone he could muster up, "I'm sorry dear. I'll make it up to you tomorrow." He had hoped his gesture would calm her for tonight, but he could tell by the glazed stare she gave him, their night was just getting started.

"Momma told me that something has been going on with you and that I needed to watch you more closely. You've been staying out late, you're always so short with me when we talk, and you ignore me in my face…." She began to sniffle. "And, and, I'm sick of it. If you're cheating, I'm giving you until the end of the day tomorrow to end it with your whore. Because if I have to go looking for her."

Paul caught her hand just as it was about to strike him. He looked at her hand like it was a disgusting and separate piece of her, and he could feel her wrist shaking.

Paul gritted his teeth and said slowly, "Sandra, I have had a rough day. Planning for this campaign has everyone on end. I'll be damned if I get bitched out there and have to come home and listen to it from my wife. Now I'm going to go up these stairs and pretend that I have a good wife." Paul's grip tightened on her wrist, and he watched her face wince in pain. "A wife that would have had enough decency to have a hot plate and pussy ready for her hard-working husband when he got home from a long day's work. One that would've called me to find out how late I was going to be so when I got home a kiss or a how was your day? Would've been the first question asked. Now I'm going to forget you raised your hand to me this one time. But you try that shit again, and you're going to wish that I just would've hit you back instead."

When he threw Sandra's wrist to the side and out of his way, she crumbled to the floor. Paul was filled with regrets and repulsion as he watched her turn into a big weeping heap.

Without giving her another look, he stepped over her still trembling body and walked towards the stairs.

Hopefully, his daughter, Christina, would have a better welcome for him. With her turning thirteen soon, Paul didn't know how much longer he had until seeing him wasn't exciting for her anymore. Then what would he do? Unbuttoning his cuffs as Paul went up the staircase, he thought about Sandra raising her hand to him. He thought about Madisin's threat. Paul couldn't grasp what was going on with the women in his life, but trust had never been a problem for them. With him running for mayor, having a reliable and secure support system is what he needed. And he was going to start building it, first thing tomorrow morning.

CHAPTER 10

MADISIN

Meet me at our spot in Cyprus Pointe Park at 2 PM. Bring Babygirl. Was the text message that Madisin had received at 7:00 AM that Sunday morning. Two things had entered her mind quickly after she read it. The first was, what fucking spot was he referring? And the second was how was he going to get out of his family day? Sunday had always been a family day for him and his wife.

*

It started when Christina was born. Every Sunday they would go to church, walk to the pier for ice cream, and eat a big catered dinner prepared by some local chef something or other. But that was no longer her concern. Paul could do or not do whatever he decided to with his wife. After a long talk with her mother, Madisin took the next week to cry and rest. She and Paul were over. Their argument that turned physical last week was the last straw. She called in on that Monday to tell him she needed time to herself, but would still work from home. Of course, as she expected, Paul didn't give her any problems. He said, "Take all the time you need baby," which let her know that his wife was not around him. It just made her even more annoyed with him. He was a fraud. She had been in love with an imposter all these years. She knew that Paul was the purest form of himself when she was around, and she loved being the one that set him free. But what good was that if he preferred to be caged. Paul allowing himself to be a prisoner to his skeletons, was making her a prisoner to him, but not anymore. Being away from Paul for that week was a fresh breath of air. Madisin found her own intelligence when Paul wasn't around making passes; telling her how much he needed her; or how much he loved her. Madisin decided that there would be no more begging him to be her man. She was not asking him anymore to be a father to her child. It was strictly business from now on out.

Madisin couldn't lie to herself, though. She did miss Paul. And to get this text from him was very much unexpected. She had handled most of whatever he needed, including having his calls transferred to her cell, from home. Even though they had minimum contact, Madisin made sure she stayed efficient by keeping his calendar updated, promptly letting him know about rescheduled meetings, and informing him of any relevant emails or calls that needed a response. If it weren't for his single "Ilu" or "Imu" texts she received from him every night, she would've thought that Paul had forgotten about them. And now this. Madisin sat up in her bed and exhaled. She had read Paul's text at least ten times since she woke up that morning, but she had not responded to him yet. She didn't want him to think that he could still make her jump whenever he got ready. Looking at the Lotus shaped digital clock on her wall, Madisin read 11:38 AM. She had about an hour before Babygirl came home from Sunday school with momma. Which means that she had only forty-five minutes to check the weather, pick out an outfit, shower, get dressed, curl her hair, and find Babygirl something to wear.

After a deep stretch and making her bed, Madisin fell to her knees and decided that she needed to spend at least ten minutes in prayer. Only God could give her the strength she needed to control her mouth and get her through this meeting.

*

Madisin and Babygirl arrived at the park twenty minutes to 2:00 PM and sat down at the small shelter closest to the water. The shelter table is where she and Paul first made love. And probably where they conceived Tatiana.

"I was worried you weren't going to come."

Tatiana jumped when she heard the deep familiar voice behind her. She raised her hand to block the sun and saw a clean-shaven and good looking Paul, standing on the other side of the table. And he had a visitor with him.

"Hello, Christina. How have you been little miss?"

Christina laughed and came and threw her hands around Madisin's neck, hugging her tightly. "I'm doing good, Ms. Foster. I missed you this week. Daddy said you were sick. Are you feeling better now?"

Smirking and looking up at Paul again, Madisin cleared her throat and gave Christina a tight hug back. "Yes, Christina. I was feeling a little down, but I'm better now."

"Good. Is Tatiana here? I missed her too!" The sparkle in Christina's eye about seeing Tatiana, her best friend, her little sister, made Madisin choke up. Those girls may never know the truth.

"Um, yes. I think she is over there looking for shells. I think she could use your help. We just so happen to have an extra bucket." Christina squealed as she grabbed the bucket and went to play.

"Aren't they cute playing together?"

"Don't you mean isn't it cute seeing your daughters play together?" Madisin regretted the comment as soon as she said it. Looking at Paul slowly sitting down on the opposite bench, "I'm sorry. I shouldn't have said that."

Paul took her hand across the table. "You know that is one thing that I always loved about you. You have never been one to hold your tongue."

Madisin scoffed, pulled her hand away, and looked out at the girls playing in the water. There was so much running through her mind and feeling Paul's touch sent a charge through her body that she wasn't ready to deal with just yet.

"Madisin, I'm sorry I brought her without telling you. It was the only way Sandra would let me out for a few hours without any problems."

Giving a small chuckle and gauging her words before she spoke, Madisin turned to him, "And you think that is okay, Paul? Do you think that is something that I want to hear after raising your child by myself for all these years? That, that, you had to use your other child to trick your wife into letting you go spend time with your side piece and your illegitimate daughter?" Sighing Madisin turned away.

"Maddie, baby. I know it sounds bad, but you know that you and Babygirl mean more to me than just that. I would never refer to you like that. And you don't give me enough credit. I helped raise Tatiana too. I know I am not there with you at night, but dammit I am there in the morning before she goes to school and I am there with you when she gets home from school and I… I help with homework sometimes. I give you both anything you could ever want. You can't tell me that you want for anything."

"We want you, Paul," Madisin said exasperated. Silence. "So where does she think you and Christina are?"

"I told her we were having a daddy-daughter day at the beach."

Madisin looked around nervously, "Oh God, Paul. Are you serious?"

Paul chuckled and grabbed Madisin's wrist before she could get up from her seat. "Maddie. Baby, sit down. Sandra is out shopping with her mother. I have it handled."

Snatching her hand away and sitting back down, "I can't believe you think this is funny, Paul."

Shaking his head, Paul grabbed Madisin's face and kissed her. For a moment, she was taken back to twenty-one when he laid her on that park table and made love to her for the first time. But the girls' giggles carried in on the wind, and her stomach dropped, and she pulled away. Peeking at the girls, she was glad to see them fully immersed in their own water activities.

"Paul, are you serious? What has gotten into you?" Madisin questioned as she scooted down the bench and held her hand to her tingling lips.

"I miss you, Maddie. You don't respond to my text. I'm lonely without you. I'm losing it without you."

"Paul don't act like I just up and did some damn disappearing act. You put your fucking hands on me. And I've stood for a lot of your shit, but putting your hands on me because you're too much of a God damn coward to see your truth is bullshit."

Trying to calm her, Madisin watched Paul put his hands up in defeat. She avoided his touch when he reached for her again.

"Maddie. Baby. You're right. I'm a coward, and I should have never, ever put my hands on you. I told you I would never do anything to hurt you and I fucked up. I fucked up royally. And I…I'm sorry. I'm just not ready to be who you want me to be yet. If I tell everyone who I am now, they will turn their backs on me. And worse, they'll probably kill me, and God knows what will happen to Christina."

Madisin came prepared for this moment. She told herself that she would remain silent and let him talk if it ever came to this, and remaining quiet was what she intended to do. She let Paul take her hand.

"I'm running for Mayor. You know like we discussed before. Baby, it's finally happening, and Barry says that I have an excellent chance of winning because of all the community work that I've been involved in with the business doing so well, and Sandra's family backing me I, I, I can't lose. Those charity projects were your doing baby. I couldn't have made it this far without you."

Madisin knew if she heard Sandra's name one more time, she was going to scream. She closed her eyes and started praying that for his sake, Paul would not make that mistake.

"I want you to come with me."

Madisin's eyes popped open and stared at Paul. "You want me to come with you, where?"

"Weren't you listening Maddie. I have a few donor meetings in South Florida; there are a few small firms that made business cases for funding in Slidell and New Orleans. After the hurricane that hit, they need help. And I need you with me."

Sliding her hands from Paul's. The cool September Gulf wind blew the sweat that Paul's palms had left on them dry.

Looking deeply into Paul's eyes, "And where is Babygirl going to be while I'm traveling?"

"Well, I can talk to your momma and have her chip in, and of course get a nanny if I need to."

"And what about your wife, Paul?"

"Sandra will be here taking care of Christina."

Madisin arched her eyebrow and gave Paul a disbelieving look. She knew Sandra liked face time. Any time that she could get in front of a camera, she would be there. And these events sounded like her type of thing.

"Well," Paul continued, "For the first month, she would be home, and when we make it to Louisiana, she would be there."

"Be there where Paul?" Madisin asked pointedly and folded her arms across her chest.

"Be there in Louisiana with us."

Even though Madisin heard the nonchalance in Paul's voice, she heard what she had to do even louder. Rising to her feet, hands now on her hip. "And are we supposed to take turns in your bed too?" Madisin turned away from Paul and heard him suck his teeth and rise from the table. She felt him approaching her and against her better judgment allowed him to wrap his arms around her. She knew it would be for the last time.

"Maddie baby. What is it?" Paul lifted her chin to meet his eyes. It was too late to stop him from seeing her flowing tears. "Aww, baby. I'm so sorry that our last argument was so bad. But I'm going to make up for it. I swear it to you. I'm going to be better for us. Just wait, you'll see."

Madisin loosened Paul's grip from around her waist and backed off the concrete slab. "See that's just it Paul. I'm not waiting anymore." Wiping the hot tears from her face, "I can't believe I waited this long."

Paul grabbed her arm, and Madisin winced. "What? What are you talking about Madisin? Do you hear yourself? Tired of waiting for what?"

Madisin refused to answer what he already knew. And she didn't want to upset the girls. Madisin tried to pull her arm away and backed into a post. "Paul, let me go, or I'll scream." The heat of Paul's breath in her face made her nervous.

"Are you telling me that you are leaving me, Madisin? Is that what you're doing?"

Turning her head away. "Paul, please let me go. You don't want to upset the girls." Madisin pleaded.

Hearing his measured tone, "Madisin, are you telling me that you are leaving me?" made Madisin want to be anywhere but where they were now.

"Paul, please. YES!" When she felt the breath leave from him, and his body went limp, Madisin ducked under his arm and looked at him with a new set of eyes. He looked like a monster. Face flushed, eyes red, breathing hard. "Tatiana! Baby tell Christina bye. Let's get ready to go."

"Oh, ma. Do we have to…?" Madisin stopped her child before she could finish, still keeping one eye on Paul, who was slowly approaching.

"Tatiana what did I tell you about talking back. Say goodbye and let's get ready to go." Paul growled,

"Madisin, you are not leaving me. You are not taking my child. I'll. I'll"

"You'll what Paul? You'll hit me again?"

"Got dammit Madisin!" Madisin snatched up her purse and threw the picture that she had wanted to give as a gift one day at Paul's face. He swiped at the air to catch it right before it hit the ground. It gave Madisin time to gather Tatiana.

"MADISIN! MADISIN!" she heard him yelling as she pulled Tatiana away to their car. "Paul, you need help. You better get your affairs in order!" "What's wrong with Mr. Christen mommy?" "Hush and get in the car girl." Madisin hated dragging Babygirl and avoiding her questions, but focusing on getting to the car was all she could do to keep her tears at bay and feel safe.

CHAPTER 11

DHORIAN

"Hey, DJ!" Dhorian heard his name called, but he didn't feel like being bothered. Especially with anyone who may have known him from this side of town.

The people he knew from this side were always trying to hold something. And he didn't have anything for them today. Dhorian doubled his pace toward the Boys and Girls club for a pickup game to try and let off some nervous energy before his big interview. He had just spent the last two days preparing for his face to face. The phone interview went well enough, but the questions they asked were harder than he thought they were going to be. He wasn't expecting questions about what Mr. Christen's company actually did.

Dhorian thought that he would find out those details while training. But sure enough, the woman asked him. The most he could get out was that Mr. Christen was the CEO of Christen Funding LLP and helped to rebuild struggling small businesses through different funding opportunities. It sounded good enough to Dhorian, but of course, the lady realized he was only doing some fancy word-smithing and told him to be more prepared in his next interview.

"Yo, DJ. Yo!" Dhorian heard the footsteps running to catch up with him and even though he wanted to run to get away from whoever this was trying to invade his thoughts, he slowed down to get the small talk over with and then he would be on his way.

Dhorian slowed and turned around to face a bent over and gasping Teddy.

"Yo, Teddy. What's up? Why you chasing me down?"

Teddy Roads laughed and said, "Ain't nobody chasing you, man. I ain't seen you since school got out and wanted to see what's up with you and if you wanted to hang out with me and the boys tonight," and then added, "while you on this side of town and all. You know you don't get out much."

Dhorian brushed off Teddy's playful nudge and scrunched up his face. He swiped his nose and laughed to himself. If he was twenty now, he knew Teddy had to be around the same age. And from what he heard, Teddy's idea of hanging out didn't just stop at basketball anymore. The way he saw it, he was too old to get caught up in any mess that Teddy and his boys had going on. He knew what kind of hanging out they did, and it usually involved some type of armed something or other, and he wasn't with that kind of hanging. Now if Teddy would have approached him maybe just a week earlier before his Paul Christen internship was a possibility, he might have taken him up on that offer. But he couldn't risk it now.

"The boys? Naw I'm straight on that." Picking up his pace again, Dhorian pulled on the hood of his jacket and shoved his hands in his pockets. He heard feet scuffle on the pavement behind him.

"Oh yeah. I meant to tell you. I heard about your cousin, man. Yo, that's foul dude."

Dhorian stopped and gave Teddy the blankest stare he could muster. He knew this is why Teddy stopped him in the first place. Over the last few months, anyone that knew he and Verdell were cousins or went to school with them at any point, stopped him to ask about his murderer cousin. They all wanted to talk about Verdell and his case. Like he could give them some inside scoop or something. Dhorian could care less about the trouble his cousin was in; Verdell or his case was the last thing that Dhorian wanted to discuss. That was Verdell's fuck up. Not his.

Sucking his teeth, Dhorian responded, "So what's it to you?" Watching Teddy stumble around for a response might have been the funniest thing he had seen in a while.

"Well. It's just that I know that your family must be taking it hard. You know, with y'all being so close and all. People used to say that y'all would run the NBA together."

"Well look how that turned out." Dhorian remarked

sarcastically. "And the family ain't taking it hard. As far as we concerned, he right where he should be. Ain't nobody tell him to kill nobody."

"Yo, I heard the chick was pregnant too!" Teddy interrupted and threw in.

If Dhorian didn't realize it before, he knew now that Teddy was pumping him for information. And if there was nothing else that upset him more, it was having his time wasted. Giving Teddy the side-eye, he decided to let him down easy, but he wanted to make sure that he wouldn't approach him with no bullshit like this again.

"Teddy. What you want to know man? Cause I ain't got no extra information for you. You heard the news and read the paper just like I did. And I usually don't like speaking on my family, but since what that nicca did was so foul I'mma tell you this, I hope they give him the chair." With a smug grin on his face, Dhorian watched Teddy start shaking his head in disbelief at his words.

"Damn man, that's messed up to feel like that about your own people. I always thought y'all was cool."

"That's what you get for thinking. And for running up on me asking me some stupid ass question about my family when you have all the information you checking me on anyway."

Hands up in defeat, Teddy exclaimed, "Look, bro, I was just trying to make sure your cousin was all right on the inside, but it don't look like you give a fuck. So you right, my bad. Apparently, the situation ain't what I thought it was. No need for the hostility. I'll catch you later."

Dhorian watched Teddy turn and walk in the opposite direction. Looking over his shoulder every few steps. Dhorian didn't blame him. He pushed out a breath of frustration and started walking again towards the rec center. He figured he had enough time to get a game or two in before he had to be back home. Just then, his phone vibrated in his pocket. Taking it out, he saw that he had five calls. Three from his father and two from Mr. Christen's office. "Oh shit." Dhorian moaned. He couldn't believe he didn't feel the phone vibrating earlier. Dhorian decided to call his father back first. He had to get his head together before calling Mr. Christen's office back.

"Yea, Pop. What's up?"

"Don't what's up me, boy?" He heard his father grunt into the phone. "What's the point of having a mobile phone if I can't reach you when you're mobile?"

"Only you would say something like that." Dhorian chuckled before responding, "My bad Pops I was on my way to the rec and got tied up talking to Teddy." Remembering what it was that he and Teddy got tied up talking about, he didn't care to go into that with his father. He already knew how disappointed his father would be at his words and didn't want to hear it. Not right now.

"What does Teddy have to do with you answering your phone?"

"Nothing Pop, I was just saying why I didn't hear the phone."

"Well, I called to see why you weren't home yet to help me clean this shed."

Clean the shed? Dhorian thought to himself. "Pop you said to be back by 4:30 to help you clean the shed and it's only…" Looking at the time showing brightly on his phone was 4:45 PM. Dhorian groaned. He didn't realize how much time he had lost. It couldn't have been from talking with Teddy, maybe the walk to the rec took longer than he initially thought. "My bad Pop. I'm on my way now."

"Yea you do that. Oh, and Mr. Christen's assistant, Ms. Foster, called here looking for you a few times as well. Incidentally, she is going on leave, and they need you to start first thing next week."

Dhorian couldn't believe his ears. "But what about the interview?"

"I guess they don't need you to do that right now. It sounded like they were looking to get somebody sooner than later because they a little shorthanded. But then again, if you would have answered your mobile phone or if you would have been in place to get the call yourself you would know the answer to these things now wouldn't you?"

"Yea, Pop. I hear you."

He heard his father grumble into the phone "mmm-hmm."

"All right Pop, I'm jogging home now."

"No need to jog now son, it's past the time you were supposed to be here."

Dhorian knew his dad was about to get into one of his rare moods where he wouldn't be able to fix his wrong no matter what he did or what he said.

"All right dad. I'm on my way. See you soon." Dhorian hung up before his father could drag the conversation further. At least he knew now what the calls from Mr. Christen's office were regarding. He had to get home and settled so he could call them back as soon as possible. Letting him do the internship without the second interview was unexpected. He didn't know what to prepare for now. Once he was home, he would be able to think better. He just had to get home first. Dhorian took off. He couldn't mess this opportunity up. If he did this right, no one would ever put him in the same conversation with Verdell again.

CHAPTER 12

PAUL

Paul held the old Polaroid instant print gently in his hands. He had been staring at the picture on and off for over an hour. When Paul came home from his budget meeting with Barry, his best friend, brother-in-law, and his campaign manager, Paul was so exhausted with all of the information that he just dropped his briefcase at the front door. He didn't even think to see if anyone was home before he locked himself in his study to make sure that no one could walk in and disturb him. If he was honest with himself, he locked himself in his office so that no one would catch him staring at the brown-skinned man and woman with the pale younger version of himself and have to explain why. There weren't many more photos like this that Paul knew of and Madisin just happened to have this one.

Paul didn't have any living relatives and was an only

child. His parents passed away in a car crash while he was in his freshman year at FSU. In their will, they left their house in Naples to him with all its belongings. But the house and everything in it was destroyed during Hurricane Opal, in '95, before he had a chance to find out if there was anything he wanted to keep. Paul had little to nothing to remind him about who he was, which made it that much easier for him to take on a new life all those years ago. It was what he feared may keep him from going further now.

Paul rubbed his thumb across the faces of his mother and father. He sniffed away the tears that had trickled down from his eyes and into his nose. They looked like they shared so much love between them. And from what Paul chose to remember from his childhood in his home, there was. He was just the son of two hard-working parents who only wanted the best for him. They couldn't have known all the pain he would experience from looking different. His pale face and burnt orange hair contrast on a significant scale to the melanin-rich skin and coiled brown hair of his parents. The slight round of their eyes that cradled the bridge of their nose was the only subtle features that they shared. But at first glance, it was tough to tell.

*

Before his parents died, Paul's "condition" made him keep to himself. He had been diagnosed with Albinism when he was born. His parents were as dark as milk chocolate, and he was born of their DNA but, was white as milk. Other than his skin paling in comparison to that of his parents, he was perfectly fine, an average healthy child by any standard. Over the years, his skin became a little more pigmented but not by much. He didn't have many friends growing up. And that was more than likely because he learned at a very early age just how cruel children could be. The ones that did tolerate him hanging around made snide comments or gave him crude nicknames like "Ghostbuster" because of how he looked. Those friendships never lasted long because Paul didn't take too well to being teased as a rite of passage to play. One time the teasing got so bad in the neighborhood, they were in, that his parents moved to a middle-class community across town where they said the kids came from "diverse" backgrounds. The kids didn't mind playing with him there, but they also had no problem ignoring him after their parents found out what he was. Like playing with him would cause contagion or something. Even though Paul had been hurt by how the other kids treated him, he still hadn't fully understood, that is until the first time he realized he was different.

He was in the fourth grade and the end of the school year dance was just a few short weeks away. Paul had already asked three girls and was waiting for them to all let him know what their parents said. With only a few days left before the dance, he was running out of time. Nearly discouraged, Paul finally opened up to his father about being rejected, convinced that his classmates would consider him even "weirder" if he showed up alone. With a lot of convincing, his old man told him to try just one more time. Just so happened that his last ask was to a tall, slim, and sassy brown-skinned girl with glasses and big wire braces. And to his surprise, Madisin Foster said yes. She was taller than most of the kids their age, and the bifocals and braces weren't exactly becoming, but Paul saw through all of that. And the fact that she said yes when those other girls left him hanging made her even more beautiful to him. From that moment until the 8th grade, Paul could only recall having one true friend, and that was Madisin Foster, his Maddie.

Looking back, Paul knew he loved her before he even knew what love was. When kids started calling him names or telling he was adopted, Madisin seemed to come to his rescue every time. She would give him a tight bear hug and say to him that the other kids were just jealous that God didn't make them unique, before socking him one in his shoulder and telling him to toughen up. When his family moved to Naples to get in on the real estate market sales, Paul and Madisin lost touch. Thinking about her made him get through the loneliness and how different he felt from the other kids his age.

By the time he went off to college, the only thing that made it easier was that there were so many people on campus that he seemed invisible. No one seemed to care or notice who he was or what he looked like. And he didn't mind it that way one bit. That all changed when paired on a case study with new student Barry Mellow in their Psych class. They worked so well together that Barry invited him over to his parent's house for dinner. He didn't realize that Barry and his family had assumed he was a white man until he found himself in the middle of a discussion about President Clinton's Race Initiative and he was asked his take on Clinton's community race dialogue. Thank God he never really had a chance to answer the question because Mr. Mellow's wife interceded at his mention of the word "savages" and all parties at the table had chimed in their input as well. His loss of appetite and shallow laughter did not deter Barry or his family from continuing to invite him over to dinner after that night and ultimately introducing him to his now-wife, Sandra Mellow. It was only when he needed his identification card to get into the members-only yacht and country club that he thought his charade would be up, but the opposite happened.

When asked for his State ID, Paul, with some quick thinking, faked like he had just recently lost it. When Barry's father, Mr. Mellow, was made aware that Paul would not be allowed membership or access without the proper identification, Paul thought all hell was going to break loose. Paul tried to leave quietly, but Mr. Mellow would not hear of it. Instead, he vouched for him with the club manager to get him in and told him that he knew a guy that knew a guy that owed him a favor who could replace his ID and any other paperwork he needed; and even introduced Paul to the guy that night. The next morning, Paul had the moonlight package white-glove delivered to his and Barry's off-campus apartment. He had only given the guy a story about how his paperwork got lost in the hurricane with his parent's house, and voila, Paul had a new State Id, driver's license, social security number, and $2000 available balance on an American Express credit card to help him get on his feet.

*

He had lived this life, very successfully, for over a decade. If anyone found out the truth, it wouldn't be from him. Paul poured the kerosene into the fireplace and lit a match. Taking one last look at the photo, Paul didn't bother to wipe away the tears as the flame took to the old photograph, engulfing it. As Paul watched the fire dance, he began to sweat as if bile was going to rise from his stomach. A stabbing pain throbbed at his temples. When Paul moved to grab his head, the pain dulled, but his head got light, and he grasped for his desk before he stumbled to the floor. He didn't even feel his head hit the ground. He didn't hear his wife's key in the door.

"Paul, Paul! Why does it smell like burning in here? Oh, Paul, are you okay?" Paul felt his wife's cold hands on his face and groping at his clothes. "Paul sweetheart, tell me where it hurts? Please tell me what to do," he heard his wife say before she began to sob uncontrollably.

How stupid can this woman be? He shouldn't have to tell her to call for an ambulance if he was laid out, barely conscious, on the floor. Any smart woman would know he was too weak to answer her, for God's sake, and probably couldn't tell them anything to do in this situation.

"Call for an ambulance. Get help." Paul couldn't remember

if he was able to finish the word help. His mouth felt so dry, and the pressure in his chest was unbearable. "Dear God," he thought, "I hope this wife of mine grows a brain and can get me help." Taking one last lucid look at the fireplace still glowing next to him, Paul hoped like hell that the picture was burnt to unrecognizable crisps if he was going to die.

CHAPTER 13

VERDELL

It had been ten months since Verdell had his heart ripped from his chest. Even if he had been able to make it to Missy's funeral, the family made it clear that he wasn't welcomed to attend. The message was sent so loud that Verdell couldn't help but hear it clear on several occasions when a few of the guards and a few more inmates decided to beat it into him.

The first time it happened, Verdell was on his way to the library for his allotted 20 minutes of free time. Blinded by a piss smelling sheet thrown over his head, Verdell took a hit to his throat, and a few more to his head and chest as he was dragged into another hallway, right in front of some guards, right outside the library, no less. Removing the ammonia smelling sheet from his head less than a minute later, Verdell found himself squinting through the darkness. Fear gripping his insides. He had seen Scared Straight and knew this was not going to end well.

Because he couldn't see or hear his attackers, he thought the best move he could make would be to make enough noise to get someone's attention. Try to scare them away even.

"Get off me, "he shouted. "Guards, guards. HELP!" he screamed. The louder he cried, the harder they hit. He screamed so loud and for what felt like so long that his windpipe began to close. Even with his mouth swollen shut, Verdell coughed up chunks of blood trying not to swallow pieces of chipped teeth. He moaned aloud, praying that someone, anyone, would stop them before they killed him. He couldn't see anymore. He couldn't hear anymore, but he could feel and just when he thought he heard Missy calling him, his body did him a favor and shut down.

They beat him into the infirmary that time. After that visit, Verdell split his time between the garden he was allowed to create while in solitary, the punching bag, and the library. The next few visits he received were less unexpected, and he made sure he wasn't the only one that left with some damage. C.O. or not. After the first six months, the attacks began to die down, and then after eight months, they stopped altogether. But he never let his guard down. He even won the last few. He smashed one guy's nose into his face with the palm of his hand, blindsided, dark halls and all. He learned to stay to himself because, in the dark, they all looked alike. Verdell would enter population from solitary or the infirmary to whispers and side-eyes. Some inmates even made a point to distance themselves from him. Verdell knew whatever word that had been passed around about him couldn't have been good. He couldn't trust anybody and was cool being by himself. It helped him keep a clear head.

This afternoon would be his fourth court hearing. He had become used to the prosecutor delaying his sentencing. He believed the suspense, in addition to the ordered ass-whooping, were a part of his punishment. What he couldn't get used to was the C.O. waking him up at 4:30 in the morning to be ready at the courthouse by 10:00 AM, and he never got used to the shackles. The iron made his wrists dark where the metal cuff rubbed. His once smooth skin was now callused. Verdell knew he was shit out of luck once Missy's family had refused his defense attorney's request to expedite the trial and sentencing. And with no money or emotional support from his father or any other family member since being locked up and going to court, he was at the mercy of the court.

As bad as the county was, he didn't want to imagine federal prison if he was convicted. He'd let the courts fuck him instead. That was better than his recurring nightmare in fed. Verdell decided he could live with the current situation. He may die in the other.

The transport ride over to the courthouse was short but crowded and painful. Men of all ages trying to give their version of a street lawyer's advice. He thought the first time he saw a courtroom would be when he and Missy were getting married.

Something small, she never liked to be too flashy or the center of attention. Verdell pushed the swelling tears across his face when he placed his head in his hands to hide his weakness. He couldn't give anyone a reason to pick him out. He couldn't take another beating.

"Hey, Hamilton? Hamilton?"

The voice rang louder and closer than Verdell anticipated because it didn't give him any time to entirely wipe his face of the tears before he was nudged with a baton to respond. Looking up cautiously, Verdell saw it was the new C.O., Lafayette, hovering over him. No one knew much about where he came from, but they did know he wasn't like the other C.O.s. Lafayette treated everyone fairly but didn't take any bullshit either. Verdell met Lafayette's eyes.

"Today is the last day of the rest of your life. Choose wisely."

Before Verdell could respond, the older inmate sitting next to him on the bench did the honors.

"Yo, Fayette. What type of shit is that to say to the young man on his sentencing day? You ain't got no encouraging words for anyone else?" Then hissed, "What type of shit is this?"

Verdell didn't even bother to respond. Looking at the guy or saying thanks or even acknowledging what he just did could have many different outcomes, none of them which would end favorably for Verdell. Instead, Verdell decided to put his head back in his hands and wait out the ride.

*

Verdell was the very last one to get out of the police van. All of the other prisoners had exited in a big group shortly after they arrived at the courthouse. Verdell didn't think anything of it, because the C.O.s sometimes gave him the courtesy of leaving the wagon last. Leaving last meant he didn't have to get piled in the holding cell with population and would more than likely be placed in a cell with little to no other inmates while he waited for his hearing upstairs. But after sitting in the freezing wagon for what he knew had to be at least 20 minutes, Verdell was getting worried until he heard Lafayette call his name.

"Hamilton. You're up."

"I'm up?" Verdell questioned. Even though his body started to move, his mind was stuck. The other court visits didn't go like this. "Am I going into holding?" Verdell asked before shivering as the wind tore through his thin prison orange jumpsuit.

Lafayette didn't answer. He just grabbed his arm, hands and feet still chained and cuffed, and lead him down the police van stairs. Chills ran up and down Verdell's back as they walked through the courthouse and passed the west wing elevator that he would usually ride down to the holding cell. He chanced a look at Lafayette but didn't bother to ask any questions. Verdell eyed the old paintings on the wall as they walked through the winding corridor. There were courtrooms on either side of him. Some were empty. Some were full. In a few of them, he could hear hysterical crying or someone screaming, mad about their sentence he presumed.

Finally, they arrived at a large brown door that read

Honorable Judge Winthrop Bentley on it in typeset gold letters. This visit was definitely different. He had never been to a judge's chamber, and he wasn't trying to be here now. Lafayette knocked and was told to come in through the heavy door. Verdell stood in the middle of the biggest den he had ever seen. Missy and her family had a nice size home, but this room had a wall to wall library, a sectional, a chaise longue, a minibar with full-size fridge and microwave, a wood computer desk and chair with a flashy looking computer on top. These were the main things that he noticed. That and the stern-faced man sitting behind the desk with a heavy black robe staring right in Verdell's face.

"Thank you, Lafayette. Can you un-cuff his hands please?"

Verdell watched as Lafayette did as told without a word.

"Thank you, Lafayette. You can leave him."

Verdell thought the C.O. was going to leave him in there by himself and his stomach dropped a little lower in his abdomen. But when he saw Lafayette stand next to the door, he breathed a sigh of relief.

"Sit down, young man." Judge Bentley addressed him.

Without a moment of hesitation, Verdell took the seat on the opposite side of the Judge's desk. He was surprised by how comfortable and plush the chair was. He hadn't sat anywhere that felt that good in a long time, if ever.

"I am going to get right down to it," the stern voice said. "It has been brought to my attention that you have experienced several hardships while incarcerated."

Verdell tried to make his face stoic at the judge's comment and was relieved when he continued without a solid response from him. He wouldn't get baited into being a snitch.

"The state is offering you the choice of finishing the remainder of your time at the S.E.L.F. correction work camp. Would you like to attend said camp or would you like to go back into the population of your own accord?"

Verdell was confused. Verdell didn't receive his sentence yet and didn't know how much time the comment, *"remainder of your time"* meant. He looked back over his shoulder at Lafayette, who was still standing at the door. Lafayette nodded at him. His words that he spoke on the ride over to the courthouse rung in Verdell's ear. *"Today is the last day of the rest of your life. Choose wisely."* Verdell looked back at the judge and gulped deeply attempting to moisten his dry mouth before he spoke.

"Yes, sir."

"Yes, sir to which son?" Judge Bentley quickly countered.

"I'll take the camp, sir." Verdell managed to stammer.

The judge wrote something down on a manila envelope and stamped it with a seal before handing it to Lafayette. Once the folder was in hand, Lafayette grabbed Verdell's arm and stood him up from the chair, placing the cuffs back on his wrist and escorting him out of the room without another word.

Everything happened so fast, Verdell had a hard time recounting what just happened. What did he agree to? Verdell noticed that Lafayette's pace had picked up and it was getting harder for him to keep up with the C.O.s stride without getting dragged a step or two because of the ankle cuffs. When it looked like they had made their way to the entrance of the courthouse where they originally came in at, Lafayette pushed Verdell through a door that Verdell hadn't noticed before. The room was dimly lit and stuffy, and Verdell's nerves were getting the best of him.

He couldn't keep quiet any longer. As soon as he was going to ask the C.O. what was going on, a sack covered Verdell's head, and he was lead back out into the cold and loaded into what his reasoning told him was a van. Body tense, Verdell waited for the beating that never came. Heard voices, not talking about much in general. His father was never really one for prayer, but he truly needed one at that moment. He did recall a prayer his mother made him recite when he would get anxious before his games and big exams. It was the only thing that came to mind. The serenity prayer.

Verdell mouthed the words in silence. *God grant me the serenity to accept the things I cannot change; courage to change the things I can; and wisdom to know the difference; living one day at a time; enjoying one moment at a time; accepting hardships as the pathway to peace; Taking, as He did, this sinful world as it is, not as I would have it; trusting that He will make all things right if I surrender to his will; that I may be reasonably happy in this life and supremely happy with Him forever in the next. Amen.*

Not having prayed in years, Verdell felt a peace wash over him sooner than he expected. Verdell felt that his prayer covered all basis as he rode toward the last day of the rest of his life.

CHAPTER 14

PAUL

"Mr. Christen? Mr. Christen? Welcome back, sir. You are a fortunate man. We almost lost you. And you had your beautiful wife here who wouldn't hear of leaving your side."

Sitting up, Paul struggled to open his eyes. His lids felt like they were being held down by weights. Once they finally peeled open, it took him a minute to adjust to the overly white bright lights in the room.

"Well sitting up on your own. That's a good sign." He heard the man dressed in the light blue scrubs and crisp white coat say. Paul assumed he was the doctor.

"It feels like I've been asleep forever. How long have I been out?" And how soon am I going to get out of here?" Paul asked. He felt Sandra take his hand in hers as they waited for the doctor to answer. The doctor cleared his throat, and Paul grew anxious by his silence. Sandra squeezed his hand.

"Dr. Weiss," Sandra started, looking at Paul with pity in her eyes, "Can you please tell my husband what you explained to me?"

Letting go of Sandra's hand, Paul cleared his throat, "Yes, Dr. Weiss, please share with me what you shared with my wife while I was out."

Taken aback by the possible insinuation, Paul saw the doctor glance at his wife under his hard stare before clearing his throat and addressing him. "Yes, of course, Mr. Christen. I'll start with why you're here."

"Please do," Paul replied snidely.

Nodding, the doctor continued. "Sure. According to your wife, you experienced a severe headache before feeling a sharp pain in your lower abdomen before becoming dizzy and passing out in which she called an ambulance. Upon arrival, the nurses noticed blood spots in your eyes, and your blood pressure was 340/135. Besides your blood pressure at dangerously high levels, there was also swelling in your feet and your ankles. When admitted, you were unresponsive, and with further testing, we were able to determine that you suffer from hypertension or high blood pressure."

Paul chuckled, "That's it? Well, give me my meds, and we are out of here. Sandra, call Barry and have him send the driver." Before Sandra could protest, the doctor continued. Paul heard the hesitancy in his voice.

"Mr. Christen, our tests also revealed that you have suffered kidney failure." Paul squinted his eyes, staring between the doctor and his teary-eyed wife.

In an even tone, Paul asked, "okay, and what does that mean exactly?"

Clearing his throat again, the doctor responded in a monotone voice, "It means Mr. Christen that you won't survive without dialysis or a kidney transplant. Do you know how long you were feeling dizzy or the sharp pains in your abdomen prior to your accident? Anything you can tell me about some of the symptoms you may have experienced leading up to you passing out can help me to determine additional tests and treatment."

Paul felt numb. The doctor's words echoed on repeat over and over in his head. *Won't survive. Symptoms. Dialysis or transplant. Treatment.* Symptoms? Paul questioned himself. He tried to recall times where he hadn't felt his best, but everything came to mind. His constant cramping, the itching on his back, but that was normal stuff. He was just dehydrated. Everyone got cramps or fatigue or dry skin. Why would he be any different? Paul heard his name called.

"Mr. Christen. It's okay if you are unable to remember anything right now. Your mind can be a little hazy after receiving this type of news."

Shit hazy was an understatement. Paul felt lost. He was at a loss.

"So where do we go from here, doc?" Paul was thankful that his wife stepped in to refocus the conversation while he gathered his thoughts.

"Well, we can go down two avenues here. The first being dialysis, which is a lifetime treatment plan. The second is a kidney transplant." Dr. Weiss looked through some papers on his clipboard before continuing. "Looking at your past health history, it does appear that you are a suitable candidate for a kidney transplant, but of course, we will have to confirm with a few more tests."

"Okay, we definitely want the transplant doc. My husband is running for office, and he needs to have the same value of life if not better after this," Sandra said before looking lovingly into his eyes.

Paul can't remember the last time she talked about him in such a caring way. At least not that he has heard.

"I like the optimism, Mrs. Christen, but I like to deal in facts. There is going to be a long road ahead for your husband. Once we confirm that he is a good candidate for a transplant, Mr. Christen will have to go through what we call the pre-transplant period."

"Pre-transplant period?" Paul asked.

"Yes, Mr. Christen. The pre-transplant period is also what we like to call the waiting game."

"I don't think there is anything gamey about this Dr. Weiss. This is serious." Sandra chided.

"Excuse the lousy humor, but it's called the waiting game for a reason. We get your name on the deceased donor waiting list while we wait for the evaluation to come back on the living donors, of your choosing, of course."

"Living donors?" Sandra asked, shocked.

"Yes, Mrs. Christen. Living donors. If you have a family member or a friend in mind that may be interested in donating a kidney, we can have them tested to make sure that they are a compatible match."

Sandra scoffed, "I couldn't imagine asking something like that of my family. My own flesh and blood."

Paul felt his head starting to pound again. He must've looked as bad as he felt. Because Dr. Weiss called the nurse in and advised that after letting his patient rest, he would be back in the morning to start the first round of testing. Paul was grateful for the break. By the time the doctor finished giving them all of the information they had needed to proceed with the next steps, Paul had thought he was going to pass out again. But his mind wouldn't let him be that lucky.

*

That was three weeks ago.

Since then, there were so many thoughts running through Paul's head. He had to get a game plan together with Barry to make sure that there was not a delay in their campaign initiatives because of his hospital stay. When he finally woke up, he had already been asleep for a week. And it took another week before released. There were at least three campaign donors and one Fortune 500 CEO that he had to call with apologies and concessions just to get them to reschedule if he even hoped to have a campaign budget.

The wait for his transplant could take longer because he needed a donor with an O blood type, amongst other things. If he couldn't keep his blood pressure down, Dr. Weiss promised he would be back in the hospital for another extended stay, prompting a dialysis regimen, delaying his campaign and decreasing his chances even more than they already were. The local news stations had already started pre-polling the entire Bay, and he was down twelve points, and Barry only thought it wasn't more because word of his illness had gotten out. Damn pity points. His wife had been tiptoeing around the house, literally, trying her hardest to make sure that she and Christina stayed out of his way when all he could hear and see was them trying to get out of his way. That may have been worse than them sticking around. Sandra promised him that she wouldn't involve his father-in-law and his connections in her search to "preserve his quality of life" as she called it. But Paul thinks she lied about that because he walked in on her whispering conversations a few times.

To top all of that off, he had an inexperienced intern and no Madisin to train him. Madisin hadn't even called him to tell him she brought somebody on and was taking time off. It's been a month, and she wasn't answering calls, she hadn't come into work, and he hadn't seen his Babygirl. She didn't even know about his kidney failure. He didn't want the last time he saw her or talked to her to be like it was the last time. But he couldn't trust her. Madisin had that picture, she had his child, she had his money, and she had his heart.

"Shiiiittt!" Paul screamed as the thoughts in his head started to make his nerves visibly wrecked. He held his shaking hands still. He couldn't let this get the best of him.

CHAPTER 15

MADISIN

Watching her Babygirl cry tears that she couldn't yet explain herself was the last straw for Madisin. When they pulled away from the park and Paul, Madisin couldn't control her emotions, let alone help her Babygirl get through hers. She knew that the more she cried, the harder Tatiana cried, but she couldn't stop herself. She couldn't stop herself because she knew that this was the end. On the ride home, Babygirl didn't say another word. She only looked out of the window, crying the entire time softly. The incident was not brought up at dinner, nor when Madisin gave Tatiana her bath, but later that night, long after her own tears were over, Madisin rubbed her Babygirl's back and sung to her quietly while she sniffled herself to sleep. She couldn't imagine what Tatiana thought that scene at the park was, but she refused to put her through anything else like that ever again. They would be just fine without Paul, and she would make sure of it.

That is what she told herself when she threw her phone in the garbage the next morning and got a new one. It's what she said when she asked her mother for help in her job hunt. That is what she told herself as she got the interview. That is what she told herself when she accepted the job offer. It's what Madisin told herself now, as she parked in the garage, and said a quick prayer before getting out of her car for her first day. It wasn't easy dodging Paul's calls and visits these last few months, but she knew it was time to let go. She could care less the lie he was living, but she refused to take part in it anymore. Good luck and good riddance. After over thirteen years of waiting, it was time for her to live for her. Madisin was so nervous that she was shaking, but her independence and Babygirl's peace was all that mattered now. Taking a deep breath, Madisin exhaled, and started her walk.

"I can do this!"

"Excuse Me. Can I help you?"

Madisin shook her head slightly to release the paralyzing fear she felt as she approached the large glass doors to the downtown central building. Her hands started to sweat as she looked up at all of the floors that seemed to stretch far into the sky.

Madisin heard the voice again, "Excuse me, Miss. Can I help you?" The high pitch Southern drawl caught her attention the second time around.

Glancing at the woman in a designer floral dress with

matching floral stilettos, Madisin slowly shook her head and said, "I'm just a little nervous. It's my first day."

"Well, you don't want to be late, right?"

Madisin glanced up at the tall building again and felt light-headed. Chuckling soft heartedly, Madisin took her first good look at the woman. She was attractive and very well put together. She couldn't have been any older than she was. Just thinking of her age made Madisin dread turning thirty-two this year. She felt like a late bloomer. It took her way too long to get over Paul and get out on her own and into the real world. But she was slowly and surely making the right steps.

"No, I guess not."

"I'm Tiffany. Like breakfast at Tiffany's, but without the "s." Most people call me Tiff. You can call me Tiff." The woman said taking Madisin's hand in hers and almost shaking it off her wrist.

Grabbing her wrist to stop it from popping out of its socket, Madisin smiled wearily and cleared her throat, letting go of Tiffany's hand. What was it with white women and grabbing her wrist, she absently thought to herself.

"Okay, Tiff. I'm Madisin."

"Oooo! Madisin like Madison Avenue or like the mermaid Madison from that movie Splash." Tiff asked excitedly and then continued, "You don't look like a Madison. Don't get me wrong, you're gorgeous, but I would have taken you for a Marsha or a Marcia. Do you know a Marsha or a Marcia? I've never met one in person, but I have met a Stephanie. She's not so pretty. Eyes are a little too big if you ask me, but you could most definitely beat her at being a Stephanie." Tiffany spoke so fast that Madisin didn't get a chance to chime in. And it didn't look like Tiffany was going to stop anytime soon to let her get a word in, so she just decided to walk into the building, and maybe Tiffany would get the hint that she wasn't interested in the conversation.

Stepping into the lobby, Madisin followed the signs to the elevators and pulled out the folded sheet of paper that her mother gave her that morning with her instructions. Pressing the "up" button and clearing her throat loudly to cut off Tiffany's tirade.

Madisin pasted a smile on her face and said, "Well, I guess this is where we part ways." Taking Tiffany's hand, Madisin shook it once and finished, "It was nice meeting you, Tiffany. Maybe I'll see you around the building sometime," and walked into the elevator pressing the button for the eleventh floor.

The cackle that followed her into the elevator made Madisin jump. She turned to face a doubled over Tiffany who seemed to be laughing way too hard. Madisin initially thought the woman was just a little too friendly when she met her outside, but now it might be worse than she thought. Tiffany could be some crazy woman. Maybe another one of Paul's women. She never knew with him, even though other women have never been an issue, she wouldn't put it past him these days. Back pressed against the opposite wall, facing Tiffany, Madisin prepared herself to either jump out of the elevator as soon as those doors opened or fight her way out.

With Tiffany's obnoxious and unsettling laughter slowing down, Madisin asked, "What's so funny?" and gave Tiffany a pointed look. It occurred to Madisin that she could have been the pun of the joke, and hoped that there wasn't something in her teeth or on her dress.

Taking a deep breath, Tiffany finally responded, "We're going to the same floor, silly."

"How do you know which floor I'm going to?" Madisin asked with her hands on her hips and a little more attitude in her voice. Not laughing anymore, Tiffany's face flushed.

"Well, I saw you push "eleven" when we got on the elevator. I just assumed that meant you were getting off on the eleventh floor. Mr. Sicario's office, right? He's the only office up there."

Embarrassed and completely ashamed of the irate sister girl act that she was about to give Tiffany, Madisin covered her face with her hands before apologizing. "I'm so sorry. It's just that it's my first day and I'm nervous. It's been a long time since I've had work other than…well work." She saw Tiffany's face crease a little at her "other than" comment, but so what she didn't owe this woman any explanations. She apologized for her rudeness, and that was that. This elevator was the slowest she had ever been on. She counted the seconds to get to the eleventh floor, but she didn't have a chance to count floors for long before Tiffany started up again.

Throwing her hands in Madisin's direction, "Oh, it's okay. There's no reason to apologize. Nobody understands first days better than me. On my first day, I bumped into Mr. Sicario's wife and spilled hot coffee all over her pretty designer dress." Giggling a little before continuing, "I just knew I was going to lose my job. I think the only thing that saved me was that it was only me and Mr. and Mrs. Sicario around. If that would've happened in front of anyone else…" Tiffany made a slicing motion over her neck with her finger and a slicing sound with her mouth.

Just then, the elevator doors opened, and the buzz of the office filled the space. Tiffany stepped off the elevator first and said good morning to almost everyone who walked by introducing Madisin as she practically pulled her along.

They arrived at a massive set of French doors, and Tiffany smiled at Madisin before hitting the intercom button that hung on the wall. "Yes," the friendly voice said from the other side.

"Morning Lola" Tiffany sung. "It's Tiff. I got Mr. Sicario's new hire, Madisin with me. She's supposed to start today."

"Ok good, she's early, but we can buzz her in."

"Thank you, Lola!" The buzzer sounded. Tiffany turned the knob to the door and hugged Madisin before wishing her luck and promising to check on her around lunchtime.

Madisin decided then that Tiffany may have been a little extra, but she was cool people. It was a big difference from what she was used to, but Madisin was happy for the change. As she walked down the long hall, marveling at the paintings and comparing how Mr. Sicario's extravagantly laid office made Paul's study look shabby, she poised her body, straightening her back and holding her head high, assuring herself again that they were definitely on their way to being just fine without Paul.

CHAPTER 16

PAUL

Paul's eyes were getting blurry as he downed his third rim filled glass of cognac. He was supposed to be preparing his final memo to the Board of Directors at his investment firm to announce his formal resignation and his decision to run for Mayor. But it just ended up being a booze and pity session.

Lightheaded and frustrated with his life, the knock at his office door only irritated him further. He told his family not to bother him. He had been real testy over the last couple of months since he and Madisin had their misunderstanding, as he would call it. And as mad as he was at her, he had to admit that he missed her like hell.

It pissed Paul off that she wasn't answering her damn phone. It was like she was trying to tie his hands. He just wanted to talk to her. To make sure that they were still on the same page. That she knew how much he cared about her. And that she should keep her damn mouth shut.

"Who is it?" Paul shouted, slurring his words and running them together. Without answering Paul's question, Barry opened the door.

"Hey, Paul I just wanted to come and check on you man. I've called your phone several times over the past week, and Sandra keeps telling me that, you know, you're feeling under the weather, and you'll give me a callback. But I haven't heard from you. What's going on, man?"

Paul looked up, frustration evident on his face. Paul slid his sweaty palm down from his forehead to his drooping lips.

"Barry, you got to help me. I don't know what else to do. Madisin won't pick up her phone. She isn't returning my calls. I drove by her mother's house a few times, but her mother always tells me she's not there."

Barry was noticeably confused by Paul's string of conversation. "Calls? Slow down. Who are we talking about here? I just saw Sandra at the front door."

"What do you mean who… what am I talking about?" Paul said, still slurring and then pointing to himself hard in the chest. "Who am I talking about? I'm talking about Maddie. Didn't you notice somebody's missing in this equation?" Paul gestured, waving his arms wildly in the messy office space around him.

Barry placed his hands in his pockets. "That's no reason to get bent out of shape. You got bigger issues. Like you drinking, while you're waiting on a new kidney." Barry said as he held up and looked through the almost empty 1.75L Remy Martin Louis XIII Baccarat crystal decanter.

Paul watched Barry pour himself a cup and sip, making swirling sounds as he moved the cognac over his lips and around his palette before swallowing it.

"Well at least you're drinking the good stuff."

Paul grunted in response.

"You got to find yourself a new secretary man. I don't know what's up with your filing system, but yeah, you're going to have to fire Maddie if she can't get it right. I don't, I don't know what else to say." And as if a second thought, Barry added, by the way, I'm looking into getting your intern trained to help you out around here and to promote your image with the inner city. I'm sure that will dredge up some points in the 3rd and 4th District."

"So it was your idea to bring this boy on?" Paul tried to shout, but it came out like a sloppy yell.

Barry sighed, irritated at Paul's drunkenness. "His name is Dhorian Hamilton Jr. His father works over there at the uh, the uh, damn. What do you call it?"

Paul shrugged at Barry's rhetorical question. How in the hell would he know? Paul watched as Barry had his aha moment.

"Funeral home! That's it. He owns his own funeral home. He saw Sandra at the store, and she thanked him for how well he did Aunt Barbara's funeral preparation and services. When Sandra asked Mr. Hamilton how his family was doing, he mentioned his son who had nothing going on for himself now but a lost basketball scholarship; and was interested in becoming a lawyer or in some kind of politics. Sandra casually brought it up a few weeks ago and thought that bringing in someone from his background for an internship or some other opportunity would be good for your image."

Paul didn't even let Barry finish. "Casually? When has Sandra ever brought up anything casually? It sounds just like something she would plot out to do. And I'll be damned if she brought you along for the ride!" Paul felt the soberness wash over him as did his anger.

Sandra was a master manipulator. She wouldn't do something unless they benefited from it somehow. He should have known Madisin wouldn't have left him with a sorry ass replacement. At least she was enough of a lady to leave him with nothing. Paul would rather her leave him with nothing than to be the guinea pig trainer for the new poster child. His new poster child. Now that he thought about it, even more, Paul had to be careful with this. The boy's background could be a Catch 22 for him. It could mean vindication or a grave situation. Paul must have been pacing for a few minutes before he noticed Barry waving his hands in his face.

"Paul. Paul. Oh man. Why are you wearing a hole in the rug with that look on your face? I thought you would be happy about this."

Paul came from around his desk toward Barry but had to steady himself and gripped the edge of the oak desk, catching himself before he tripped. Somehow the vision of he and

Maddie's last romp played like an HD video in his head, and the sensation ran cold through his veins.

"Barry, I need to tell you something."

Barry leaned against the bookshelf and folded his arms. "Okay, I'm listening."

Paul blew out a deep breath. "I think Dhorian will work out fine for the campaign, but I need you to hear me when I say there is no campaign if she doesn't return my call."

Barry was lost. The creases in his face grew deep. "There's no campaign? The hell you talking? I've been working for months on this. Setting things up. Getting investigators and people you know to talk to the community, to share your vision. What do you mean no campaign? I got everything riding on this. We got everything riding on this. And you're talking about some phone call?" Barry slapped the desk. "You got to start making some sense."

Paul almost felt bad for not telling Barry this before. He had put in so much work, but this could not only ruin their chances to win the campaign, it could hurt their family, and most importantly, their friendship. Paul wouldn't be who he was today without Barry. If nothing else, Paul owed him the truth. He just didn't know how much of it he would be okay giving him. Paul gave Barry a blank stare. He was thinking of what to say.

"Paul, do I need to get Sandra in here to call your doctor or somebody."

Paul quickly shook his head. "No, no, no need to do that."

And then exasperated, "its Maddie. I'm talking about Madisin. You know the brown skin woman that we have in here? You know the one that's been my secretary for the past eleven years?" Paul could see Barry's impatient glare, obviously wanting him to move the story along.

"Yeah, yeah, I know. What? What about it?" Dhorian just told me that she was sick when I asked why he answered the door instead of Madisin."

"Yea, she told me her mother was sick and needed time off." Paul let the lie slip from his mouth with ease.

Barry shrugged at the unwarranted bit of information. "Yea, her taking four months off for being sick is terrible. But I told you that I have someone coming in to train Dhorian next week and he should be able to help you out with your filing system. But why does that have to ruin the campaign? It's just not making sense to me."

"Madisin she is," Paul paused and swallowed the last of the cognac in his glass and enjoyed the burn that coated his throat. "She is more than just my secretary Barry."

"More than just your secretary?" Barry asked, trying to search Paul's eyes for what he wasn't saying. And then Paul caught the light bulb in Barry's "you sly dog" stare.

Paul knew when Barry started his light chuckle that grew in loud cynical laughter that he knew what 'more than just my secretary' meant.

"I know what you mean. She is a nice piece of ass. I mean I would think that you know, you were hitting that. But I didn't know that we had to discuss it. Why the hell would you mention that to me?"

"Well, that nice piece of ass and I have a child together."

Barry put his hands up in the air, and immediately, Paul knew he was stepping outside of their comfort zone. Letting Barry in on this truth was a huge risk, but he needed help.

"Whoa, whoa, whoa! Slow down! This is getting hot! Like you couldn't baby-step me into this information? I think I'm going to need some of that Louis." Barry strolled over to Paul's dry bar and picked up the crystal decanter and took a big swig, throwing the liquid to the back of his throat. After he swallowed, Barry's eyes got big, and he slapped himself on his chest a few times before letting out a big belch. "Whew."

Paul stared at him, blankly.

"Now start from the beginning, Paul. I'm trying to take this all in." Paul let Berry put it together in his own words then. It would be less of a chance of Paul stumbling over his words or telling too much if Barry filled in the gaps of the story himself.

"So you're telling me Madisin, your secretary for the past eleven or so years, is not only the woman you are having an affair with, but you also have a little pickaninny with her too Paul? No wonder you're in here drinking and going crazy that's she's not calling you back. She could wreck everything. Fuck just the campaign. And you couldn't keep your dick in your pants. Why did you have to tell me this now? I mean, we all like chocolate, but SHIT!"

Paul watched as Barry began to pace the office. His hands

were going from folding across his chest to massaging his temples. Paul knew all too well the type of headache that Barry must have been experiencing at this moment.

"This one hits too close to home. Does Sandra know anything about this?"

Paul jumped up from his relaxed leaned position against his desk, "No she doesn't so if you can lower your fucking voice and maybe we can keep it that way, and I can at least try to save my marriage and my goddamn image."

Barry's tense face slackened and started to look at Paul with pity in his eyes.

"You're right. You're right. Okay, so let's start thinking about damage control. So you say you can't get in contact with her? Let's put a private investigator on her and see if we can locate her and talk some sense into her." Barry took another swig of the cognac. "I mean, what did you do to make her mad enough to avoid you? Did you not pay your child support? Like what's happening?"

"Well," Paul breathed a heavy sigh. He was hoping Barry wouldn't ask this many questions, but he did just tell him that he had an affair on his sister that resulted in a love child, so he owed him some type of response. "I told her I was going to run for mayor and told her that I wanted her to come travel with me while I'm out touring for the campaign."

Barry surprisingly seemed more intrigued than upset at this information, "Okay. Possible family time. That sounds promising. What seems to be the problem with that?"

"For one, she's not too happy that Sandra's going to be on the trip too."

Barry shook his head. "Damn! Just a regular old Playboy. Right now is not the time to have your cake and eat it too, Paul. We have to think smart about these things. I wish you would have talked to me before you decided to have a conversation with her. Now she can ruin us with this, this love child thing. I mean it, it's a little child, right?" Barry held his hand next to his knees for emphasis. "Maybe we can spin this. Maybe it's not your child. Maybe this pickaninny is someone else's bastard spawn."

"Now you hold on there! You're not going to continue to talk about my child like that." Paul sputtered, surprised at the strength of his voice.

Barry continued sarcastically, "oh good! At least you love the child. Have you met the child?"

"Yeah, I met her. She and Christina play together all the time." Paul tried to avoid the shock and disappointed look on Barry's face.

"I mean, I don't know what to say right now, Paul. It sounds like you got yourself in a right pickle."

Paul realized he was losing Barry. His only true friend, and maybe his only ally in getting this mess with Madisin cleaned up. He had to take control of this. Had to get Barry back on his side. Even if he had to guilt him into it. Hands-on his chest and with all the accusation he could muster in his voice, "I got myself? Oh no, now I'm in this alone? What happened to you being my campaign manager?"

Barry was not taking the bait, just yet. "Well damn it. I don't know Paul. Right now it sounds a lot like you're managing the buffet at your own damn affair. I can't help if you don't tell me. If you don't let me in. I mean I could have given you some other suggestions and ways to handle this other than the way that you did."

Reigning him in, Paul dismissed his last statement, "Okay well, what's done, is done. Can we start with finding Maddie?"

"Okay, I want you to find out what's going to be the plan from there because I refuse to let my whole career go down the damn toilet because you decided that you want to be with a black woman and her baby. No offense."

"You know Barry, just because you put your hands up and say no offense doesn't mean that the situation and your comment is still not offend-able."

Barry put his hands down. "Well, that's all I can say on short notice." Taking his handkerchief out of his breast pocket and wiping the sweat off his face, Barry continued, "Dammit it's a lot to take in at one time."

Paul watched Barry shuffle through his dry bar in frustration, placing everything to one side and then the other.

"Are you sure you don't have anything else harder to drink in here. I need something to help wash it all down. Something to help me think straight."

Barry had turned up several nearly empty decanters and onto his waiting tongue, trying to get the last drops from all of them. After the fourth decanter, Paul walked over and snatched it from Barry's hands.

"Damn it, Barry. I need you to get your shit together. I need your help."

"Okay, well I may know somebody very highly recommended to help us with your little problem."

"Help us how? Paul asked eyebrow raised. "What? Help us to find Maddie? Okay well, that there's a start. I say let's go with that." Paul rested his hands on his hips. "Let's talk about costs."

Barry laughed at Paul's naiveté. "You don't talk about costs. With these people, you get what you pay for."

Paul shrugged his shoulders absently. "I only meant that I don't care how much it cost. I just want to make sure that she's delivered to me without a scratch on her.

Making his move towards the door, Barry grabbed a stogie off Paul's desk, "Right, I'll go ahead and make that call now."

Feeling more relaxed, Paul straightened some papers on his desk and sat behind it.

Before Barry could get out the door, he looked back at Paul and asked, "Is there anything else that I need to know Paul?"

Centering himself and looking him straight in the eye, Paul got back out of his seat and rounded his desk towards his friend of over 15 years and put his hand on Barry's shoulder. "Of course not friend," and closed the door behind him.

CHAPTER 17

DHORIAN

Running through the cold hard rain with donuts and Dunkin coffee at 9:45 in the A.M. was not how Dhorian imagined his morning going. It wasn't even how he envisioned his first job going — especially working for someone as connected as Mr. Paul Christen. He hadn't even gotten a paycheck yet, and he knew it had to be at least two weeks since he started. This internship shit, or working for the free shit, as he called it, was quickly becoming for the birds, the worms, and the rest of the critters.

There were too many rules and not enough perks. Where was his morning donuts and coffee? His catered lunch? His tailored suits, expense card, and driver? Mr. Christen was living the life, and Dhorian could not wait until his lifestyle kicked in too. Well, who was he kidding? What was his alternative? Staying at home and being forced to clean out old sheds and attics?

A late-night cleaning out the shed is what had him running late this morning. He practically had to beg his father to let him go to bed at 11:35 PM, and he still didn't fall asleep until well after 12:30 in the morning. When he finally woke up, his body ached all over. He hadn't hurt like that since conditioning last season. And when Dhorian saw what time it was, his head began to ache too. He was going to be late again. The only thing he came out on top with was his mother's diary; it fell out of an old cardboard box filled with pieces of clothing that hadn't been sewn together yet. His mother was a seamstress and found joy in taking pieces from old clothes and sewing them into new ones. She had always had her own style with mixing patterns and fabrics. Dhorian missed his mother so much. So when he saw the old book with the small lock fall, he didn't even tell his father. Dhorian wanted to keep this possible piece of her to himself. It took him over an hour to get the little lock off, which is the other reason why he was running close to an hour late in his slacks, button-up, and tie soaked and trying to keep rainwater out of Mr. Christen's latte.

Dhorian ran into the Christen residence and tried to tiptoe by Mr. Christen's study to the kitchen to warm up his latte before he was spotted and called out on his lack of punctuality, but the woman's voice coming from Mr. Christen's study made him stop in his tracks. Dhorian noticed the door was cracked and walked closer to it. The aggressive voice made him put his ear closer to the door.

"I don't care where you take her or what it takes. Well,

I'm not paying you to ask questions. I'm paying you to get it done. He is not on his death bed. Yes, she'll be there. Because I had her followed. He doesn't have much time. I need it done sooner than later. You would like to be paid sooner rather than later, wouldn't you? If I'm not paying you to plan and execute than why the hell am I paying you? It has to be done this way. Over SEVENTY THOUSAND people are waiting for the same thing my husband is waiting for, but I bet you their asses aren't running for mayor. Are they? My husband will be the next mayor. This is the only way. I will not wait for my husband to be a statistic. I don't want him treated. I want him cured. What do I care what you do with the body? Just make sure it's done right, or you will have other arrangements to figure it out. I hope you have your affairs in order."

Dhorian didn't realize he was holding his breath at what he had just overheard until he realized that his exhale made him lean a little too much into the door. The woman must've heard the door creak because Dhorian heard the loud noise the phone made when it disconnected the call.

Wanting to get to her before she made it out to confront him, Dhorian quickly burst through the door, "Mr. Christen sorry I'm late, I have your coffee order. You wouldn't believe that they gave me decaf to make your latte instead of... Oh hello. You're not Mr. Christen." Dhorian gave Mrs. Christen, who he recognized from the family painting in the hallway, a surprised look that he prayed was convincing enough.

"You think? Who are you? And how long were you standing

in that hallway before you decided to barge in so rudely."

"Oh, I'm sorry." Dhorian said quickly placing the cup holder with the single coffee on Mr. Christen's desk. He wiped his sweaty palms on his crisp suit bottom, leaving a wet print, before putting his hand out to shake Mrs. Christen's hand and introduce himself. "My name is Dhorian Hamilton. I'm interning for your husband."

He wasn't surprised to see the look of suspicion on her face or that she hadn't yet shaken his hand.

"Do you always enter rooms before knocking?"

"I do apologize Mrs. Christen, but Mr. Christen and I usually have our morning debriefs in here before his morning meeting starts. A deep voice boomed from behind him making Dhorian jump.

"And you were late. Why?" After trying to play off his initial alarm, Dhorian had never been so relieved to hear Paul's chastising voice.

"Sir, Mr. Christen. Good Morning. You wouldn't believe that they tried to serve you decaf in your latte sir?" "Is that right, Mr. Hamilton?"

Dhorian glanced at Mrs. Christen, who was not enjoying her interrogation disrupted one bit. "Uh, yes, sir."

"Your father called me about ten minutes ago and asked that I excuse your tardiness because you were assisting him with a chore that you had been putting off for a while now. Is that right son?"

Chuckling nervously, Dhorian responded, "Uh, yes, sir."

"Well, three things. One. I don't like tardiness. Two. I hate liars. Three. Procrastination is a sin." "Are we clear on that Mr. Hamilton?"

Dhorian watched, mouth open as Mr. Christen looked through his mail and other documents while ripping him a new one. He couldn't recall ever being made to feel so small. And his father had mastered that skill. "Yes, sir. I understand sir."

Coming over and touching him on his shoulder and giving him eye contact. "Good then. If you are going to be my protégé, we have to break bad habits, and I'm going to start by teaching you good business acumen. Sound good?"

Dhorian's eyes grew at the idea of being Mr. Paul Christen's protégé. Hell, he was going to be the next mayor for God's sake. Of course, it sounded good. It sounded great. Nodding his head and responding, "Yes, sir, that sounds like a plan."

"Great. You can start by throwing out that coffee, because not only were you tardy, but it is now cold." It wasn't until Dhorian moved to throw the coffee away in the small trash can next to Mrs. Christen that Mr. Christen noticed her still standing there.

"Good Morning, babe. I'm sorry I didn't notice you still standing there." He went to kiss her on her cheek. Dhorian saw the fake smile she plastered on her face as she stared into his. Dhorian quickly averted his eyes. "Do you and Christina have anything planned today?"

Breaking her stare from Dhorian, she replied, "No dear.

Nothing you should worry yourself with. I'll let you, men-folks get to your politics. Remember to take your meds and call me if you need me, darling."

Without looking at her to respond, Mr. Christen responded, "Yes, love. Will do. Please close the door behind you."

Nodding and making her exit, Dhorian couldn't help but lock eyes with her again. After she was gone and the study doors closed, Dhorian was still watching her.

"Dhorian! Dhorian!" He heard Mr. Christen's voice raise the second time he called him. Dhorian looked at Mr. Christen. It was obvious that he had checked out on the conversation and needed to be brought back up to speed. Mr. Christen did not look moved. "Young man. So far, I have not been impressed with what you offer as an intern and am seriously thinking about changing what I said about you being my protégé. After this internship, you walk out into this world a mirror of me, and I do not tolerate laziness, indecisiveness, or having one's head in the clouds. This life may come with some perks, but it is not for everyone. If you do not think you are ready, then please do not waste the opportunity, my time, or your father's good name."

Sure that he had lost his chance and determined to prove himself, Dhorian straightened his back, stiffened his shoulders, looked Mr. Christen straight in his eyes, "Mr. Christen. I apologize that my head has been in the clouds lately and that I haven't been taking this opportunity as seriously as I should have. But I want this life, sir. I want respect. And I'm willing to do anything it takes to get there sir. If you give me another chance, I promise I won't let you down."

Seemingly satisfied with his plea, Mr. Christen rounded his desk and stood in front of it, making Dhorian take a step back. "Anything it takes, huh?"

"Yes, sir," Dhorian echoed. "Anything it takes."

Mr. Christen turned abruptly and went back behind his desk, taking a seat. "Good, we have a 12:30 meeting with Barry to discuss campaign budget. I need you to grab a pen, paper, my laptop, but after you run out and get me a hot non-decaf latte." Dhorian looked at his watch. He only had 30 minutes to make it across town and back in lunch hour traffic. "Shit," He mumbled. "Shit is right." Mr. Christen chuckled before checking his watch and saying "Anything" as he walked out the door.

CHAPTER 18

VERDELL

Verdell walked onto the Buddy Dodge show floor. "Hey. Can you tell Donovan I'm here?"

Being the only customer in the car superstore right outside of Bartow at 8:00 AM, it wasn't hard for Verdell to pick out the salesman. Not at all surprised by the salesman's look of confusion, Verdell looked at the name tag and addressed him again.

"Uh, Victor, is it?" Verdell pointed at the well-dressed man with the heavily oiled comb-over. He watched Victor look down at his name tag on his jacket to check his name. "What's wrong? You forgot your own name?" Verdell chuckled.

Embarrassed, the salesman straightened his jacket, cleared his throat, and replied, "No, sir. How can I help you today?"

"You can help me by telling Donovan he has a man here to see him about a dog."

A look of unease crossed over Victor's face. Verdell didn't blame him. He thought what this could have looked like from his point of view. A 6'2 muscular black guy dressed in a fitted short sleeve button up, surfer shirts, open-toe sandals, aviator shades, and hair knotted on his face and head walks into an auto store known for shady dealings and overpriced luxury vehicles and asks for his boss's boss to come to see him about a dog. Verdell had to laugh because he could only imagine what could be going through Victor's head. The guy looked like he didn't know if he should be afraid or amused. But Verdell also saw that he wasn't confident enough to try either card. Good for him. Verdell decided to put him at ease just a little.

"Don't worry. I'm leaving in a car too." Verdell assured Victor making eye contact with him over his Aviator shades and giving him a full smile complimented by 32 pearly whites and a wink. Some of the tension visibly released from Victor's shoulders as he relaxed, but only a little.

Hesitantly, "Let me check with my manager to see if Mr. Belasco is in yet, and I'll be…uh right back to see if you need any help picking out a vehicle."

Verdell nodded and turned his back to take another look at the cars on the showroom floor before Victor turned to leave. That didn't stop Verdell from hearing disgruntled Victor clearing his throat and mumbling "do I look like a fucking messenger?" before tugging at his jacket sleeves and turning away to go do just that. Deliver his message.

Twenty minutes later, when Donovan Belasco found Verdell

in the showroom, he was sitting behind the wheel of a pearl Navy blue, HEMI V8, five-speed automatic, 2008 Dodge Challenger. It was only October 2007, and the model hadn't released yet, but Verdell knew he just had to have it. And he would before he left.

"You must be who they sent?" A gruff voice asked in his direction.

Verdell heard the sound but didn't see the face.

"You don't look like the others."

Verdell stared at the massive shadow of the head peering at him through the small gap of the tinted window. Verdell barely glanced at the swollen face man, trying to avoid the smoke and the heat that his stogie pushed into the window.

"I think that was kind of the point, don't you?" Verdell asked Donovan slyly.

Verdell opened the door without warning and saw the big man take a few steps back from the force before he stepped out. Verdell had to look up into the chubby bulldog face to see into the puffy black and dilated eyes of Donovan Maurice Belasco. A 6'7 retired door to door salesman who found his niche selling a few cars that fell off the back of a truck 30 years ago and strong-armed it into an empire. Verdell eyed him up and down. If Donovan Belasco was the thug that Verdell had researched him to be, things were going to get interesting. He cleaned up pretty good. The Coogi jumpsuit was a way better look than the prison-issued Orange jumpsuit he saw him in. Verdell spotted movement out of his peripheral.

In front of him, Victor was locking the customer entrance and exit doors to the showroom. Four men came from around the car dressed in black suits and ties. Visibly armed, they stood behind Donovan Belasco, facing him. Verdell thought to himself, how corny could this guy be? Who still had official bodyguards that actually dressed like bodyguards? Had he never heard of a goon? At least a goon would have the element of surprise.

Removing his aviators and tucking them in the pocket of his button-up, Verdell put his hands up in surrender, "look I'm only here to deliver a message. And I've been advised to advise you not to shoot the messenger."

Verdell watched as Donovan Belasco and three of his non-goons all began to laugh loudly. None of their laughs were louder than Donovan Belasco.

Looking at Verdell in contempt, he countered, "You've been advised to advise me? What type of shit is this? Who did you say you were?"

Verdell detected the heavy Boston accent. Just a minute ago, he would have sworn the man was authentic Italian. He must've made Donovan Belasco mad because his façade was starting to fall and his tell was starting to show. Too bad he was nowhere near as furious as he was going to be by the time Verdell was through him. Verdell almost felt bad for them, but not really. Getting under skins was his specialty. Hands still up in surrender, Verdell only looked at them. He gave them all a good once over and knew each one's size, dominant side, and gauged their weaknesses. He could sense the intensity growing in the room.

"Do you want the message or not? If you like, I can deliver it to your wife instead. I got outstanding white-glove service."

Donovan Belasco was the only one in his crew who snickered this time. Although Verdell saw the laugh, he heard the threat in it. Two of his men stepped closer to him. Donovan Belasco halted them with one wave of his right hand.

"Let him speak. I'll say if we shouldn't listen to his advisement or not." He ordered as he stretched the syllables in advisement. As requested, the men halted, guns still drawn. Verdell had seen a Skorpion and an Uzi already but wasn't sure what else they were packing. Clearing his throat, Verdell began to recall the message from memory:

"Dear Donnie, I bet you were hoping to hear from Chino. But Chino's dead. I had the guy that is giving you this message kill him for me. Chino couldn't tell me why my money or my delivery was short. But after a few fingers went missing, he told me to come ask you. That was before Vee cut out his tongue. I don't want to bore you with details. Bottom line, Chino didn't make it. I want you to make it, though. Tell my guy, Vee, where my money and my delivery is, and I'll let him tell you where he buried your wife. Don't let me down, Donnie. It's too late for your wife, but your life depends on it."

After Verdell delivered his message, he relaxed, arms down crossed in front of him. Not one ounce of stress or fear detectable. He was in his element, tension and pressure. He let the silence build for a few seconds knowing that they needed a minute to digest the severity of the message. Verdell almost timed it perfectly when all hell would break loose.

"What is this some fucking sick joke? Off this black beach boy looking, mother…" The last of Donnie's words were cut off by the sound of bullets ricocheting and firing off in his direction.

Of course, more guns were firing off than he saw, but Verdell came prepared for this. He ducked behind the car. He was mad as hell that his new car was being shot up, but he knew a guy that knew a guy who could fix it up, brand new.

"Donnie, I see you are not too happy about the message," Verdell yelled over the approaching gunfire.

They were coming for him. He reached under the back of his button-up and grabbed the two flashbangs he brought with him for just this occasion. Verdell crouched behind the rear bumper of the vehicle and risked getting shot while gauging his targets. Throwing one on each side of the car, Verdell heard the men scream. He didn't have long to finish his work before they gained consciousness.

*

Verdell snapped his fingers three times. "Time to wake the fuck up Donnie. You've been out for a while, and I've been busy."

Verdell saw Donovan Belasco stirring. He couldn't wait for him to wake up and see all the fun he had without him.

Verdell sang, "Donnie. Donnie. Time to get up."

Clapping two bricks together in front of his disorganized vision finally did the trick and made him come to. Donovan Belasco had the look of pure terror plastered all over his face. His eyes were shifting side to side, taking in the scene. Verdell knew he read his body language accurately because he saw the floor flood with urine beneath him.

"Yo, my man. That's some nasty shit. But since this is your place, I mean they did it." Verdell swept his arm across the room to show off his fallen soldiers. "Do your thing."

The sweat began showing through Donovan Belasco's clothes. His neck and chest soaked. Face perspiring.

"I know this looks bad, Donnie. Really, I do. But I have to be honest with you. It's going to get worst."

While Donovan Belasco was sleeping off the effects of the flashbang and the strong sedative Verdell injected him with, he dragged the five unconscious bodies, one by one, to a back warehouse in the showroom.

At the same time, Donnie slept, Verdell questioned and tortured his men. Salesman Victor was the first to wake up and was beaten mercilessly. The other three non-goons regained consciousness just as Verdell was finishing off unlucky Victor. He had made the sale but, unfortunately, wouldn't get his commission on that day or any other, for that matter. Breaking jaws by smashing a skull on a concrete floor at full force takes effort, and sounds a bit like knocking at a door. Their reaction was what he expected. Everyone started talking at once before Verdell had the chance to ask his first question. Each of them dished more dirt than the last, begging for their life. But Verdell was there for a job. And his job was not done. He never left a job undone.

By the time Verdell finished with Donovan Belasco's henchman, the warehouse room was a mess. It reeked of piss and hot feces. Not to mention, the blood and a few body parts that splattered against the walls and floors in the room surrounding them.

Verdell found out way more information than he was hired to do. There was one thing for sure. Donovan Maurice Belasco was a nasty, grimy, mother fucker. And in his opinion, the man's wife was better off dead than living with a scumbag like him. Not only had Donovan Belasco been stealing money, dope, and cars from his connect and benefactor, but he also had a thing for drugging little girls and sampling them before he sold them off to the highest bidder. This dog deserved worse than anything, Verdell could give him. But Verdell was determined to give the thieving predator his best shot.

Now strapped to a desk, Donovan Belasco was face up, head, shoulders, and knees hanging off the ends. Verdell left him a little slack in the rope to give him a sense of hope, but only to destroy whatever ideas of survival remained in his head. Donovan Belasco was so busy taking in the scene when he had awakened that he didn't realize his own state. Verdell had been taking his time with him. He had numbed Donovan Belasco's face, hands, and feet. After he finished with the others, he started slowly working on their boss. First, he used a cigar cutter to clip off his fingers and toes at the knuckles and joints. With Donnie heavily sedated and his limbs and face numb, Verdell didn't have to worry about the excessive screaming or having unnecessary scuffles while he cauterized the amputated parts.

Verdell used Donovan Belasco's right index finger and pointed it at him.

"I know you want to scream Donnie, but just a warning, if you do you may choke to death."

The large rose gold ring with the diamond engraved initials, D.M.B., that sat at the knuckle of the finger caught Donovan Belasco's eye. The moan that came from his throat was guttural.

"Oh, stop crying. You can't feel that." Verdell mocked. "But you will feel what I have planned for your disgusting ass."

Verdell didn't think it was possible, but Donnie's eyes grew bigger. They looked as if they were ready to pop out of the man's head.

"Oh, yea. I know all about you." Verdell said, still pointing his finger at him accusingly. "You've been a real sleazy, slimy individual. Do you know that? Money, drugs, and cars sound like the life, but it turned my stomach when your men told me that you had a taste for little girls." Verdell paused for effect. "Notice, I said had?"

He watched the tears fall from Donovan Belasco's bursting eye sockets. His moans were more intense.

"It's a place in hell for men like you. Your wife thought so too right before I pulled her tongue from her throat. It turns out you weren't such a nice husband to her either." Donovan Belasco's head shook wildly. His body was lurching to get loose.

"Whoa, you're going to hurt yourself before I get a chance to."

Verdell placed Donovan Belasco's finger in a tin box with the others he had collected. He walked over to a chest on the other side of the room and pulled out leather gloves. These gloves were his special gloves.

*

They took everything he had that made him who he was on that bus leaving the prison, which was very little. When Verdell first arrived at the work camp, he was in isolation for 45 days; thrown into a makeshift room with only two concrete walls and exposure to the elements. Elements that only took him days to realize were human-made.

They gave him sunlight and freshwater the first two days, but nothing was predictable after that time. On day three, he woke up freezing, white snow surrounding his cot out as far as he could see and a pair of leather gloves at his feet. There was no food and no clothing, other than the linen pants and cotton top he wore when thrown in. They kept it snowing and cold until he had used the gloves to dig up an aloe plant he had remembered seeing in his first days to cover his blistered lips. That was day 5. He had not eaten anything for five days, no sunlight for 3. He passed out in the snow after finding the aloe and awoke to a tropical paradise.

Verdell couldn't understand the change in his surroundings, but he soon learned that he was in a test facility. And even though he couldn't see anyone, he was being watched. With every challenge he completed, they took away more until all he had left were the gloves and flora and fauna encompassing the ever-changing space around him.

Naked and broken, Verdell began to build himself back up with the details that remained unchanged. He healed himself with aloes. He identified the poison fruit and used it to catch the wild game. It may have taken him a few trial and errors, but he remembered enough from his dual-enrollment, study plant toxicology class to keep him alive. The gloves weren't the same from those days, but they embodied his love for plants and the value of life. They personified his passion for discovering fruits, weaknesses, and defenses.

At the work camp, Verdell realized that just when he thought nature was at its most vulnerable; it was also at its most defensive; it's most dangerous. The beauty of danger is what Verdell loved about studying plant life.

*

As he snapped the gloves at the wrists, Verdell told his victim, "I usually don't take this long to kill someone, you know? But it's something about a fat, arrogant, thieving, abusive, and pedophiliac bastard that gets under my skin."

Verdell pulled out a vial filled with a yellow milky substance from the chest-box. No bigger than his hand, but far more damaging, Verdell walked the concoction over to Donovan Belasco, who hadn't stopped squirming, eyes still bugged with fear.

Showing Donnie the vial, "you see this Donnie? This little concoction is from the hippomane mancinella or the manchineel plant. One drop of the juice from this plant usually causes nothing more than an allergic reaction. Something like dermatitis."

Verdell shrugged, hinting at its simplicity.

"But for you, I created something special. I concentrated the manicheel and added a little bit of this and a little more of that. For your benefit, of course." Verdell teased. "Donnie, Donnie, Donnie stop crying. It's over for you. I am what happens when you live your life without the fucking fear of consequence or consideration." Verdell stopped pacing back and forth. "I am here to give you both."

Verdell could tell that the numbness was wearing off on Donovan Belasco's face because his moans were starting to sound more like pleas.

"If you survive this, note that I said if. You might want to get you some more henchman. May I suggest goons? If you don't know what a goon is, it's still your blues brothers band you had out there, but less visible more loyal."

Verdell removed the Damascus steel blade from his waistband and cut a square in the velour fabric at Donovan Belasco's pelvic region. With all of Donnie's thrashing, he almost cut him prematurely.

"Yo Donnie. Do you want your dick cut off? What the hell is wrong with you bucking like that? You know that's what got you here in the first place?"

Donovan Belasco was able to whisper the word, "please" out on his raspy brittle voice.

"Don't beg Donnie. It's not becoming of a boss like yourself to do so. Wait you didn't think I was going to cut your nasty ass pecker off did you?"

"No, no, no" Donovan Belasco managed to stutter out while shaking his head vigorously.

Waving his gloved finger at him, Verdell charged, "oh yes, you did."

Positioning the vial over Donovan Belasco's exposed flesh, Verdell began to pour the milky substance into his lap and continued until the vile was empty.

"I wouldn't let you off that easy."

The burning smell that rose from the chemical reaction had caused Verdell to gag. The pain must have been intense because Donovan Belasco's hoarse scream was interrupted by chunks of yellow bile that spewed from his mouth and involuntary muscle spasms. Verdell watched as the flesh peeled back from the muscle, and instant blisters bust after the puss in it stretched the small area of skin to capacity. Donovan Belasco had the look of death in his bleeding eyes. Who would have imagined this was the option he chose, but it was sure as hell better than prison. Verdell removed one of his gloves to check the pulse.

"Goodbye, Donnie. And good riddance."

CHAPTER 19

MADISIN

Today was a day of bad Omens. Even though Madisin said the Lord's Prayer as she had done every morning since she decided to turn her life around and quit Paul for good, everything still seemed off. The prayer usually gave her peace through her worst anxiety attacks, but there was a lingering tightness in her chest and an uneasiness in her stomach that began to shroud her like a shadow when she woke up this morning.

Her car wouldn't start, and it was a 45-minute wait for roadside assistance to come out and replace her battery. She wasted coffee on the breast of her new pink dress as she was walking into work from the parking garage. The printer ran out of ink just as Mr. Sicario needed his agenda printed out for his next meeting. When she finally replaced the ink and toner to print, her computer gave her the ominous blue screen of death.

Thank God she was working on the agenda with another woman in the office and she was able to print the copies, but by the time she made it to the meeting, the agenda print out was no longer needed. Not to mention the look of annoyance and disappointment that Mr. Sicario and his colleagues gave her.

Then the shawl she found in her trunk to cover the coffee stain on her dress was accidentally dunked into the toilet when she sat down to pee before leaving work and was no longer hiding her stain and to add insult to injury, was now soaked with urine.

Her only relief and saving grace for the day was that she had already planned it to be a half-day. She and Tiffany were going to leave work early to pick up Babygirl and take her shopping for her birthday. Tomorrow was Tatiana's twelfth birthday, and Madisin refused to let anything get her down. But she had to admit; it was on days like this that she thought about Paul the most.

At first, she was like a feign and thought about him every day. He was deep in her veins like an itch that couldn't be scratched. And then Madisin would get down, disgusted with herself even, for still feeling like that about him. It was Tiffany who gave her the idea to disconnect from him completely after she caught her in the stairwell bawling. Madisin didn't tell her who he was or all the details, but the sob story was relatable enough, that Tiffany empathized and invited her out for drinks after work.

They had nothing in common. Madisin had a child, and

Tiffany didn't have any children. Madisin had been strung along for eleven years, and Tiffany hadn't had a stable relationship in about the same amount of time. Tiffany came from money but moved to Tampa from Norfolk, Virginia when she was only 18 to make her own fortune, and Madisin, even though she was blessed enough to save a mini treasure, had come from less than modest means. With nothing common in their backgrounds, they still enjoyed each other's company. And Madisin considered Tiffany to be a friend.

*

There were many nights she laid restless, embarrassed at how stupid she was to think that she and Paul could ever have something real. When she was honest with herself, and those candid moments happened more and more, she realized that Paul was a complete asshole. No eggs, water, oil, or mixing needed. As far back as she tried to think, he treated her like some object that he owned. He always put work first. He never spoke to her in complete sentences unless it was about sex. He was controlling. Sometimes he ignored her if only to get a reaction. It was damn near impossible to work for the man and remain professional on those days. Looking back on it all, Madisin didn't know how she made it through. She never felt like he wanted to know how she felt about anything. In a few words, Paul made her feel stupid. Like she couldn't be herself. And for the first time in a decade, Madisin was loving being in her skin. She was not answering to anyone and was becoming her own woman and reaching her full potential. She and Babygirl would be all right. Who Madisin felt terrible for was Sandra.

*

Madisin exhaled sharply. "This day couldn't get any longer," she said to no one in particular as she walked through the lobby annex towards the garage to wait for Tiffany to finish her shift.

Even though it was 45 minutes to 1:00 PM, the dim lights in the garage and the concrete walls made the open space feel like midnight. Madisin could hear the metal from the inside of her stiletto heel-clicking and scraping against the asphalt. The noise was a little eerie. For it to be lunchtime, she noticed that the garage was empty even though filled with so many cars.

Maybe they were having another office potluck, she thought to herself. But the entire building wouldn't be in on that, right? She laughed at herself for being so silly. She was making something out of nothing. She finally reached the elevator and checked her watch before entering. Madisin never realized how long the walk was from the office to the garage elevator. A full 8 minutes had passed. No wonder her calves were burning.

Riding up to the seventh floor, Madisin used the ride to plan the rest of the day mentally. She wasn't nervous when the lights in the elevator flickered the first time. But on the fifth floor when the elevator jerked just a little, and the lights flickered, she thought she was going to start hyperventilating. Madisin gripped tightly to the rail and wrapped her other arm around her queasy stomach to try and hold her nerves. She practically jumped out of the elevator on the seventh floor. Madisin watched the elevator light flicker again as the doors closed.

Turning to walk towards her car on the furthest side of the garage, Madisin grunted out her irritability at the long walk in stilettos, but the car wasn't going to come to her, so she started walking. She heard the eerie clicking of her heels again, but this time there was an echo that sounded like it was right next to her.

Madisin chuckled again at being so silly for letting her work herself up into being afraid of nothing, but still, she picked up speed. The sound of the electricity pumping to the lights over her head seemed to get louder. The crackle sounded like an insect getting trapped in one of those electric blue bug zappers. The lights flickered. Madisin looked around her to see if there was anyone else noticing the weird lights and maybe they could buddy system to her car, but there was no one. She distinctly heard two sets of footsteps. She even stopped to see if the other footsteps would keep going. Maybe they were on the other side of the garage, which is why she couldn't see them. But nothing. She shook her head at the thought that she was going crazy. She was finally cracking under all the pressure she had been under lately.

But crazy or not, Madisin knew what she heard and what she saw, and she was not going to be crazy out in the open. She even thought about asking if anyone was there. But no need in asking questions she already knew the answer to. Someone was there, and Madisin knew it. She would be just fine finishing her breakdown in her car.

Madisin took out her key fob and chirped the car alarm. She saw her car. It wasn't too much further. Then the lights in the garage went out. All of them. It was like someone hit a big light switch. The system whirred as if winding down and Madisin stood still. Now completely terrified. There were those footsteps again. Her heart dropped into her chest, and she took off running for her car.

"Jesus. Jesus. Jesus," she breathed out the closer she got to her car.

Madisin kept pushing the key fob to set the alarm. She hoped whoever was following her wouldn't beat her to her car. When she reached her car, she grabbed at the driver door and realized that she hadn't yet unlocked it. Looking down at her key fob to make sure that she was pressing the right button, she finally heard the door unlock, and she jumped into her driver seat in one motion, locking her car doors with one button. She was breathing so hard that her chest burned. She couldn't move just yet. Madisin knew she was too worked up. She tried to bend her head in between her knees to calm herself, but her head only made it as far as the steering wheel.

Knock, knock, knock. Madisin jumped. There was a figure at her passenger door, and she felt paralyzed. Madisin stopped breathing. Whoever it was wouldn't see her if she stopped breathing and stayed still. The banging on her passenger window came louder. *Bam, bam, bam.*

"Just leave me alone!" Madisin screamed. "Go away."

The lights came back on the garage all at once, and Madisin saw who it was. Tiffany looked just as terrified as she was. Madisin unlocked her car door to let her friend in.

"Girl, what in the hell are you doing? You scared the hell out of me." Madisin said out of breath and starting to giggle away her nervousness and fear from the moment before.

"Girl did you see those lights go out. I had to run to the vegan place on Tyler St. for one of Mr. Sicario's people and came through the South part of the garage. The lights went out on me in the garage on my way up here, and I damn near had a fit."

Madisin stared at Tiffany's pale face, flushed red with sweat beads ruining her makeup. They both had a good laugh pulling themselves together before Madisin pulled out of the garage.

*

"Mommy, my tummy hurts."

The change in demeanor and the pain she heard in her daughter's voice made Madisin stop in the middle of her conversation.

Looking at her daughter wearily, Madisin asked Tatiana, "is it really bad baby? We are almost done shopping. Mommy and Ms. Tiffany only have a few more things to grab for your party tomorrow."

Tatiana held her arms across her stomach and moaned nodding her head yes. And then to add emphasis, she pointed to where it hurt. "It hurts in this area, mommy."

Madisin saw where her daughter was pointing and knew the cramps gripping her Babygirl would not allow her to finish their grocery shopping.

"Oh, baby. Are you keeping up with your planner? Do you need to go to the bathroom first?"

Solemn, "No, mommy, I just want to lay down. My stomach hurts, and I feel like I'm going to throw up."

Madisin shook her head at how her daughter was carrying on. The curse on the women in her family with intense period pains made Madisin leary of accusing Tatiana of faking. Madisin just doubted they were as bad as Tatiana was putting on. That little girl was growing into her own big personality right in Madisin's face. They had been going from store to store in the mall since 2:00 PM looking for things for her party, but as soon as the outing didn't directly benefit her, she fell sick. She got that self-serving trait from her father. Madisin sighed, grabbed her Babygirl's hand, and looked at her watch.

"Tiffany, I think that'll be all the shopping we get through today. I guess I'll have to call out tomorrow to get the rest of the groceries I need."

"No, ma'am. You will not call out tomorrow. You know how Mr. Sicario feels about employees that call out on Friday."

"Yea, yea, yea," Madisin mumbled.

"If you're out unplanned on Friday, don't plan to come back on Monday." They both said, each trying to mimic their version of Mr. Sicario.

"Mommy!" Tatiana whined.

"Babygirl hold on a sec."

"Mommy, I'm not a baby. My name is Tatiana. How many times do I have to tell you?"

Usually, Madisin would have found her daughter's correction cute and would have refuted with "as long as you live, you will always be my Babygirl." But she was not in the mood for the dramatics today. It had been a very long day, and she still had more things to do. Just as she was getting ready to leave the buggy and walk out of the store in a huff, she heard Tiffany speak up.

"Why don't you let me take her to the car? I can sit in there with her."

Madisin didn't mean for her face to reflect the "hell naw" that she was thinking, but it did anyway. Good thing Tiffany knew her well enough not to take offense.

"Okay, wait, hear me out. You can't call out tomorrow, especially with the day you had today. Babygi… I mean Tatiana" Tiffany cut off and recouped her thought at the side-eye that Tatiana gave her and then the smile and look of approval once she called her by name. "Tatiana isn't going to make it if she is cramping as bad as she says. The last thing you want is a cleanup on any of these aisles if this girl vomits."

Madisin did think Tiffany had a point and slackened the "this better be good" lean she had when she placed her hand on her hips just moments before.

"You only have a few more items on the list, right?"

"Yea I guess you're right." Madisin reluctantly replied.

Taking the keys from Madisin's hand, Tiffany and Tatiana speed walked out of the store and to the car. Madisin was a little relieved to see her Babygirl wince while laughing on her way out the door. At least she knew she wasn't faking entirely.

Madisin couldn't believe Tatiana was turning twelve already. She was such a young lady. She had started her cycle the night that they came home from Cypress Pointe Park. It wasn't a complete shock to either of them, because Madisin made sure to stay transparent with her daughter about everything. Well, almost everything. But Madisin was not going to let her mind go down that road for the second time today. If Paul didn't want to be in their lives, in Tatiana's life, that was his loss.

Twenty minutes later, Madisin exited the doors of the storefront with her hands full of bags. It was just her luck that the sky had up and decided to change that morning's sunny and dry day into a cloudy one that was on the verge of a torrential storm from what she could see. She wasn't sure what had the whole city of Tampa in this particular grocery store, but there wasn't a cart in sight for her to put her grocery bags in to make the long trek to her car just a little painless in the coming rain. It wasn't a full-blown storm yet, but she could smell it coming.

"Well ain't that Florida weather for you. Damn."

Madisin shook her head and cursed as she bent low and used her knees to push the three oversized paper bags securely back into her arms. Annoyed at the crowd of patrons standing in line for the only three registers open and the amount of time it was taking the clerk to come back with plastic bags, Madisin was offered the paper ones and settled for those.

As if hit by an invisible brick wall, Madisin stopped instantly right in the middle of the parking lot. Ignoring the angry acoustics of several car horns, she stared blankly at her car that was still halfway across the lot and prayed that the feeling now sitting in the pit of her gut was not because it suddenly came to her that she had no idea where her damn car keys were. Determined to not go back into that clustered muck of a store, Madisin groaned and looked back over her shoulder at all the people still hustling in and out. That was confirmation enough that going back into the store would not be her first option. She would never find her keys in there. Too many steps had already walked over her own for her to retrace them. And in this neighborhood, she would be lucky if someone returned her name if she lost it, let alone her keys. Just thinking about it made a cold shiver snake down her spine.

Realizing that she might have spent twenty seconds too long in the middle of the road weighing her options, Madisin started to walk again carefully maneuvering the weight of the bags from leg to leg as her hands rummaged through them. Suddenly she remembered that she gave her keys to Tiffany. Madisin palmed herself on the forehead and continued her struggle to the car.

"Hey, beautiful. You look like you struggling there. Can I give you some help?"

Madisin couldn't remember the last time she saw a man this

fine. She felt her jaw open and immediately closed it when a drop of rain cascaded down the top of her lip and onto her tongue. She laughed, thinking about how she must've looked like some thirsty dog in heat to him. She shifted her bags and tried to get her thoughts together, but the lips that traced his smile had her speechless.

"Here let me get that for you." The man reached out to grab her bag of eggs, pasta, bread, and flour.

"Ummm" Madisin cleared her throat. "Thank you." "Sure thing beautiful. Now, where are you parked?"

Madisin stared a little bit longer at the man, gauging his tight smooth chocolate skin, his knotted hair and beard knotted but neat and tapered like the younger men wore these days. Madisin guessed he couldn't be older than twenty-five. With a new perspective, she was finally able to control herself.

"Beautiful? Boy, I'm old enough to be your mother."

Given, if he was twenty-five, at best she could have been an older sister, but Madisin wanted to make sure that he knew that she saw the gap between them and wanted to establish that he had not one chance in hell of fulfilling any cougar fantasies with her.

"I'll only let you be my momma if I can be your daddy," his sly voice said.

Madisin giggled and blushed at his slick remark. If her hands weren't so full, she probably would have popped his shoulder or something.

"Are you flirting with me?"

"I was just trying to help a beautiful woman with her groceries is all."

He had deep dimples that pinched his cheeks and made his smirk look so damn sexy. Madisin shrugged over one of her bags to the fine ass man.

"Damn momma, what you went shopping for bricks?" He chuckled.

Madisin chuckled with him and quipped, "I'm sorry, daddy. But momma cooks. I know you may have a hard time lifting anything other than a happy meal for your little girlfriends."

There was that smirk again. Madisin turned and kept walking towards her car. The man ran up behind her laughing hard.

"That was a good one."

"Oh, you thought so?" Madisin said coyly.

The closer they got to her car, the quieter Madisin became. Something didn't look right. Something didn't feel right. She still heard the guy next to her talking, but she hadn't listened to a word he said. Everything around her seemed as if it was moving in slow motion. She focused on her car. For a moment she wanted to run towards it, but she was stuck. Madisin couldn't move her feet. The confusion that held her in place turned into a fear that gripped her chest.

Her car doors were open. The door ajar notification was chiming loudly. Madisin swore she saw a body lying on the ground next to the passenger side of the car. Madisin dropped her bags and ran over to her car to peer in the open rear driver side door. Other than the seatbelt stretched out; nothing looked out of place at first glance. Then Madisin saw it. On the ground in between the passenger rear door and the seat. The thin chain and silver heart pendant with her, Tatiana's, and Paul's initials on it. It was the only thing he ever gifted his daughter.

Panic burning in her chest, Madisin looked around the filled grocery parking lot and screamed, "Tatiana. Tatiana. Babygirl, its mommy. Please, dear God."

Running around to the other side of the car, Madisin screamed at the sight of Tiffany laying stiff, partially in and out of the front passenger door and unmoving. Madisin slowly stepped closer to see if she was still breathing. The tears began to flow when Madisin saw all of the blood on Tiffany's face. Madisin put her ear to her mouth and thought she felt a wisp of air, brush past her cheek. It could have been the wind from the coming rain, but Madisin needed to find her daughter. She shook Tiffany and turned her around to a sitting position so that she could get a good look at her.

"Tiffany! Tiffany!" Madisin said a little louder while shaking her shoulders forcefully. "Tiffany, where is my baby? Where is Tatiana?"

Madisin gasped when she finally heard Tiffany moan. Madisin finally saw where all of the blood on Tiffany's face came from when she moved her bangs. It looked like Tiffany had been bashed in the head. Hard. Madisin could see bone through the exposed meat on the finger wide gash at Tiffany's temple.

Tiffany coughed, and blood gushed out of the opening.

"Oh, God." Madisin reached into the glove compartment and grabbed all the napkins she could reach and pressed them against Tiffany's forehead. "Shit. Shit. Shit." Madisin knew that Tiffany wasn't going to be any help. "Please someone call for help. I need an ambulance."

Madisin couldn't believe that there were people crowded around her, but no one was moving.

"My daughter is missing. Someone, please call for help."

Madisin's throat was burning. It was becoming hard for her to breathe. Wait. Where was the guy that was helping her with her bags? Maybe he could help her. Madisin pushed through the gathering crowd looking for the handsome young man that was helping her before. To Madisin's surprise, the young man was nowhere around.

It wasn't making sense to her. Madisin finally began to break down. She was nothing without her daughter. Nothing was making sense to her. She felt herself breaking. Everyone that she trusted with their lives had gone. Momma was going to kill her for losing her granddaughter and trusting strangers with the well-being of her child. *"You never really know anyone that well"*, her mother always said to her. Madisin sank in the parking lot and cried. She had finally lost it. And everything with it, including her daughter.

CHAPTER 20

PAUL

It had been two months since his health scare, and Paul had managed to keep his blood pressure down. He was trying to do everything in his power to not end up back in the hospital. Paul even made the doctor or his nurse practitioner perform his follow-ups and appointments at his home. Paul had made it up in his mind that he was not going back to that place unless it was for the transplant that he so desperately needed. He even had a night nurse to come and assist him with his cycler machine while he slept at night to make sure he could still attend his meetings and run his business during the day. But his spirits were high. Just earlier in the week, at his last appointment, Dr. Weiss told him that he made it on the UNOS deceased donor waiting list. He didn't even care to ask how long that would take. It was another step accomplished.

Paul figured he had other things to keep him busy while

he waited. He still had so much going on with getting the intern trained and all of the debate preparation. It became a full-time job in itself just to assure Sandra that he was okay. He felt terrible that he was so short with her most of the time, but he couldn't help but feel like she always had an angle. It could be the simplest thing, but it didn't change his suspicions about how attentive she had been. Sandra hovered before, but her hovering now just made him feel like he was sick and on his death bed or something. There was also the issue of Madisin. Paul still hadn't heard from her. Would she care that he was sick? Would it make her change her mind about leaving him and come back to him if not for work then for love?

"Ppppff love" Paul scoffed out loud.

Good thing the morning paper was in front of his face or Sandra, his hovering wife, might have inquired about what he was referencing. And he highly wanted to avoid that conversation. As much as Sandra disliked Madisin, it definitely showed when she stopped working for him. Sandra didn't even question her absence. And that was fine with Paul too. Another conversation he didn't mind avoiding. Sunday mornings had been designated family mornings for he and Sandra ever since Christina was born. But the older Christina got, the less he saw her on Sunday mornings, and he almost resented being left alone with Sandra.

Ring, Ring, Ring. Ring, Ring, Ring. Paul never answered the phone on Sundays. It was his off day. Everyone knew that, even Madisin. She had his cell phone number which had not changed in the time that they had been together. So if she wanted to call him, she could have.

Ring, Ring, Ring. Ring, Ring, Ring. Paul and Sandra's eyes met.

"I'm not getting it. You know I don't take calls on Sundays."

Sandra huffed her frustration and got up from the kitchen table to answer the nostalgic cordless phone on the wall. Just as she approached it, the phone stopped ringing. Sandra eyed the phone before turning a cold eye to Paul and starting back towards her morning blueberry muffin and knitting at the table.

Ring, Ring, Ring. Ring, Ring, Ring. The phone rang again right before Sandra's rump hit the chair.

"Well," Paul looked at her incredulously and said before snickering to himself. Whoever that was on the phone was making his day. He knew stupid things like this irritated Sandra beyond belief, and he enjoyed seeing her flustered.

This time Sandra made it to the phone, but she still missed the call. Paul watched her stand for a few seconds near the receiver anticipating it ringing again, but it never did. Instead, there was a red light that blinked on the bottom of the phone base. Sandra lifted the phone from the receiver and pressed the blinking messages button. Paul thought he heard a high pitched woman's voice that sounded a bit like Madisin, but he dismissed that notion as soon as he thought it up. Sandra would be down his throat about him receiving a call on Sunday, from Madisin at that. Paul watched Sandra put a finger to her ear as she listened to the receiver.

"Paul? Paul? It's Madisin. I've been trying to get in contact with you for over a week, but I didn't have your cell phone number and had to look up your home number. I know I shouldn't call, especially on a Sunday, but it's important. I wouldn't call you unless it was important. Someone kidnapped Tatiana last week. They took her from my car in the grocery store parking lot. The hospital called me a few hours ago to tell me they have her Paul. Thank God they had our baby. But...but...but when I got to her, they said she was missing a kidney. Paul, did you hear me. Our baby had her fucking kidney taken. The police think it's a part of some type of organ stealing ring or some mess like that. Paul? Paul are you there? Can you please come to Brandon Regional when you get this? I'm scared, Paul and our baby needs us. Room 321..."

Paul didn't hear the other line. He only saw Sandra's face smirk in amusement. Whoever it was on the other line was a woman and was surely excited about something. Paul stared at Sandra as she placed the phone back in its base and sauntered back over to where she was sitting at the table, a smug grin plastered on her face.

Paul took a bite of his veggie omelet before asking her, "So, who was that?"

Sandra only smiled wider and said, "Hmmm?" like she didn't hear his question.

Paul considered maybe she didn't.

He took a sip of his tea, cleared his throat, and asked enunciated his question, "I asked, who that was on the phone."

The sharp look on Sandra's face was driving him crazy. He noticed her fidgeting and her hesitance before she responded.

"Oh, honey, that was no one."

Paul knew when he was being brushed off.

"What do you mean that was no one? I practically heard the woman coming through the phone."

More fidgeting.

"Well. I wanted to find a way to deliver the message to you. I didn't want just to come out and say it. I wanted to surprise you."

"Well, you have my attention now. Just tell me now!" Paul was getting annoyed. "Is it good or bad? If it's bad, give me that news first. That way, I have something to compare the good to when you tell me."

Sandra chuckled, "No, silly. That is great news."

"Ok! So tell me already."

Sandra's excitement had Paul taken aback. "It was the doctor's office baby. They found a donor!"

Paul was in shock. That was certainly good news, but why wouldn't she just come out and tell him that. He had just gotten the word that he had made it on the donor list last week. He wasn't sure how the waiting process worked, but he couldn't believe he had gotten the call this soon. Finally, out of his stupor, Paul had so many questions that he wanted to ask. His growing excitement made him stand up too.

"Are you serious? Are you sure that's what they said?"

Sandra appearing more comfortable now with her

responses, answered, "Of course I'm sure. I wouldn't dare play about something like that.

"Wow. Okay. Sooo next steps?" Paul said to no one in particular. Before Sandra had time to interject, Paul rushed over to the phone to call the doctor's office back for what he needed to do next.

Unfortunately for him, "Wait!" Sandra shrieked. "This good news has me so excited that I am in the mood for a little…" Sandra didn't complete her sentence.

Instead, Paul watched as she went down to her knees and began playing with the opening of his cotton pajama bottoms. Paul couldn't remember the last time he and Sandra were intimate. Paul had grown to strongly dislike making love to Sandra. Her idea of lovemaking was slow and sensual. Very slow and not sensual. At least nothing that he considered to be sensual. Or even sexy for that matter. Her slow was the pace of a sloth and nothing as graceful. Under normal circumstances, any man seeing his wife going down to her knees for oral would usually go gaga, Paul assumed. Their manhood rising to the occasion, but not Paul at least, not for Sandra. Their circumstances were anything but normal.

Paul groaned.

Sandra must have mistaken his annoyance as a moan of anticipation because Paul heard her mumble, "I know baby. It has been a while with everything going on, but with you being sick and everything, I want to show you how much I appreciate you."

Paul threw his head back, irritated at the monologue. Even with his semi-hard penis in her hand, she made him feel weak. And like he owed whatever strength he would or could have to her. It was just like Sandra to not know when to just shut up and get to it. Everything didn't need a damn introduction. Just get to it already.

Once again, Sandra thought his gesture was his eagerness for her to continue. She gripped his penis tightly in her hand and spread her fingers as far as they could go. Paul could see Sandra gathering saliva in her mouth. She placed sloppy spit glob puddles disguised as kisses in between the gaps of her open fingers. When done, she looked up at Paul with a sly smirk on her face. Paul had already covered his face with one of his hands to hide his amusement. For some reason, Sandra always did this instead of actually putting her mouth on his shaft before jacking it.

Sure enough, she began to move her hand up and down. Paul exhaled as the good feeling warmed in his waist. When Sandra covered the head of his hardening shaft with her lips, Paul trembled. He would have bet money that his wife would have never sucked his dick and handled it at the same time. That was a Madisin thing. A vision of Madisin gagging on his shaft sent a shiver through his back that intensified when Sandra's wet lips finally made it over his helmet. She played with the head of his penis by sucking it in her mouth slowly and pulling off it so that it made the Blow Pop "popping" noise every time. At the same time, Sandra squeezed her hand from the bottom of Paul's penis to right below where her lips played.

Damn, Paul thought. It only took her close to fifteen years before she got it right. Maybe if she had learned how to suck his dick sooner, Madisin wouldn't be…Paul cut off his thought. Who was he kidding? He and Madisin were in sync in every way. Every way but the one that she…

"Oh shit." Paul said out loud. He didn't know the exact moment when Sandra took him out of her mouth, but now she was perched one knee on the kitchen table, the other on the breakfast bar stool. He chuckled to himself as Sandra gave him another one of her sensual smirks over her shoulder. Her house dress was pulled up over her hips, exposing her untanned and pale ass. But her moist, bright pink center was all that Paul needed to see. It took him a minute to read Sandra's gesture as permission to enter.

Sandra rarely let him enter her from behind. Maybe this was a sign she was going to give their lovemaking an upgrade. With all that he was going through, he did deserve it right? Paul inserted himself slowly, just like he knew Sandra liked it. And even though her body caved receiving about half of him so far, she made not one sound. But her body was responding, so Paul continued to push the rest of his still not all the way hard erection inside her.

Even though he was currently screwing his wife, Paul chuckled to himself at the memory of how hard he would get with Madisin. If in this same position, she would be begging for the rest of his thick shaft to punish her chocolate mound.

Paul shivered at the thought. He felt Sandra go still. She was probably afraid that Paul was going to ram her, but Paul knew better.

Earlier in their relationship, he allegedly "stroked her too hard" and Sandra threatened to call the police or get him counseling if he ever did it again. It took them weeks to have sex after that incident, so Paul avoided it. And though he was far from enthused now, he had to admit that having his dick wet was a nice change to the drought he had over the last few months because of Madisin's stubbornness. Paul ground his hips back and forth, holding Sandra by her waist and making her body rock with him. Maybe this time would be different. Paul decided to test his odds. He moved one of his hands from Sandra's up to her side and around to cup her breast.

Paul considered himself to be a breast man, but Sandra wouldn't have known that if he advertised it on his forehead. She had a perfect set, but never let him explore them. If he didn't have Madisin, he might have held a grudge about that. He loved the way breasts melted in his hands; how the areola and the nipple would tighten and harden at the touch of his hand or tongue.

Paul let his head fall back, not out of annoyance this time, but out of ecstasy. He almost felt bad that sex without Madisin felt this good. Paul moved his other hand to Sandra's other breast and didn't increase the speed of his stroke, but he changed the force that his hard shaft thrust to her walls. Sandra still did not make a noise. It didn't bother Paul. He was in his zone. Paul began to roll his wife's hardened nipples between his thumb and forefinger.

He was surprised when she abruptly slapped his hand and shouted, "NO," moving his hand back to her waist.

The stinging pain threw Paul off his game, and he almost slipped further inside Sandra but caught himself on the corner of the kitchen table. Thank God he was able to avert that disaster. Sandra would have put him under the jail for going that deep.

Now came the awkwardness. Fully turned off, Paul kept his stroke while he wrestled with his thoughts. Wasn't there a better way to communicate during sex? He wasn't some dog that needed training. The awkwardness was loud in their silence. It was so quiet he could hear his thoughts loud and clear. The only noise in the room was the wet smooshing of their bodies. Sandra's reaction and her overall blandness made it no longer desirable. Hell, he had more excitement jerking his own dick reminiscing about him and Madisin's escapades.

Paul had drawn the line at not getting "his" in the past. If he went that far, he was at least going to see it through to his end if nothing else. Paul couldn't remember ever faking an orgasm in his life. However, this session was pushing that line. With Madisin, he always wanted more for as long as she would give it to him. Sandra, on the other hand, was what he considered to be vanilla. And at this moment he wanted anything but vanilla. Paul knew he was going to hate himself for this later, and he decided to deal with his destroyed record then.

Paul began growling and placed his hand in the middle of Sandra's back. He jiggled his stroke a few times before shouting "Ahhhh!" and shaking his body with enough intensity and a few hard thrusts that he almost fooled himself into believing his own act. He quickly pulled out his wet and limp penis and shoved it back through the hole in his pajama pants. Rubbing the cloth of the pants over his stickiness to adjust for sensitivity, Paul turned to the fridge before Sandra could say anything to turn him off more.

Opening the freezer, Paul looked over at the slack-jawed Sandra like they were not just in the throes of sex and said, "I got a taste for chocolate ice cream, how about you? Want anything?"

CHAPTER 21

DHORIAN

Between helping his father at the funeral home and training to keep up with Mr. Christen, Dhorian had finally been able to afford a car, a 2007 snow white Chevy Malibu. Nothing too fancy. It had a few years and some mileage on it, but it was his. And it gave him hope that if he could get a nice car for himself in just a few months, in a year who knew what luxury vehicle would come to his door. Dhorian found himself taking his lunches in the car because if he didn't make himself scarce, Mr. Christen would damn sure find him something to do. Dhorian appreciated everything he was learning, but he was not trying to overwork himself before his time. And he couldn't afford to be late coming back from lunch, so the car it was.

It was during this time that Dhorian had been reading bits and pieces of his mother's diary. There were so many things he found out about his mother that he didn't know. In every page, it was like he was meeting her again for the first time. He never knew that his mother and his aunt Annemarie were so close until around the time he and his cousin were born. His mother didn't mention why they stopped talking, only that they had, but Dhorian kept reading to see if he could find out. He wanted to find out all he could about his mother. And today, he got more than he bargained. It was like his mother was writing a message, Dhorian just didn't know to whom.

Entry date, June 28, 2001 - *Tonight he asked me if you were his and I couldn't tell him no. The words they wouldn't leave my mouth. But my eyes couldn't keep the secret. He saw right through me. He always could. And I couldn't hold onto it any longer. Please forgive me. I thought that one day, God would settle my spirit and give me peace for what we did. For it was out of love that you were born and out of love that you were given. It was a good thing that we did. Your aunt and I. Your mother and I. She only wanted what was best for you, and I promised that I would keep you safe and never let anything happen to you. But he knows. I don't know how, but he knows that you aren't his. No matter what I say to try and convince him, he tells me I reek of sin. I have never sinned in our marriage. I have never sinned against you.*

Dhorian felt his chest close in on itself. He would have considered it good writing for a TV drama if it wasn't his life. Who the hell is she talking about? Dhorian asked himself. It wasn't making any sense. He didn't have any sisters or brothers that he knew about. Not even the bastard kind, so the shit had to be about him. Dhorian flipped through the pages rapidly, flipped the book upside and shook it wildly, looking for the rest of the story. There was nothing on the remaining pages. That entry was the last among the blank pages. A single tear hit the withered page of the notebook.

Dhorian had started the car without a second thought and was on his way home to get answers. Checking the clock on the dash, he knew his father was at the funeral home. When he pulled up to the brick red old cigar building, Dhorian ran from room to room looking for his father. He was still too confused by the words he had just read to call out to his father. Was he his father? What in the hell was going on? The more Dhorian looked through the rooms in the main hall and then upstairs, the more upset he would get. His skin burned in a cold sweat as his thoughts ran feral in his mind. He was filling in the truth that was missing with his assumptions. He couldn't imagine what in the hell his mother was talking about. His father had told him that his mother had gone crazy towards the end and he did remember her being a little distant with him, but he knew for a fact that she would never take her own life. And she sure as shit wouldn't have written something down like that unless she meant something by it.

His anger was helping him to find his voice, "Pops! Pops, where are you?" Dhorian yelled out.

"I'm downstairs." He heard a faint sound call back. Hearing his father's voice made him still.

He loved his father and didn't know what he was getting ready to walk into. He didn't want to make his father feel guilty about anything. All Dhorian wanted was the truth. He tried to pace himself and prepare for any response he would receive. Dhorian inhaled a sharp slow breath filling his lungs, and then exhaled in three short bursts. He repeated this three times before going down the stairs into the embalming room.

"Hey boy, why are you not at work? It's good to see you. Can you come, give me a hand?" His father asked, not even looking at his son as he handled the cadaver.

"Dad?" Dhorian called for his father's attention.

"Yea son, could you grab the feet there and …"

"Dad!" Dhorian called again. Getting his father's full attention as he slammed his hand on the work table.

"Son, what the hell is wrong with you?"

"I am hoping that you could answer that for me. What is this?" Dhorian hadn't meant to come off so forceful, but if he hadn't gotten his father's attention, he would have helped his father through the full preparation and beautification process without getting his questions answered.

He watched his father wash his hands twice before toweling them off and walking towards him. As much as he felt like he needed to be held up at that moment, he didn't want it to be his father who did it. Not at that moment. All his father could do for him at that moment was give him the truth.

"Let me see what you got there, son."

Pulling it back from his grasp, Dhorian backed away again.

Seeing his father's uncertain gaze made him feel bad, but this was a horrible moment for him, and all he wanted was the truth.

"What the hell is wrong with you, Dhorian? You look like you've seen a ghost. You need me to call somebody?"

Instead of answering his father's questions, Dhorian began to read the entry from his mother's diary. As he read and looked up to gauge his father's reaction in between his words, hot tears spilled from his eyes. Dhorian knew the words held some truth before he could finish reading. But he had to see this through. Dhorian read the text right until the very end. When he finished, it was his father who looked like he had seen a ghost.

"Where did you get that? Where did you find that?"

Dhorian just stared at the man who had raised him and had been more to him than he could voice at that moment.

"Are you, my father?"

"Yes. Of course, I'm your father. What would make you ask me such a stupid question like that?

"Isn't that the same stupid question you asked?" Dhorian quipped.

Remembering the entry said that his father had once asked if Dhorian had belonged to him.

His father stammering, "Now, now you hold on there. You don't know anything about what your mother and I went through. I loved," Dhorian watched him gulp those words down hard, "I love your mother, son."

"Don't call me that!"

"What the hell you mean don't call you that. I raised your ungrateful ass. And I don't give a damn what you found. I am your father, and you will respect me."

The hot air forming in Dhorian's chest was burning him alive. He didn't know what he was feeling. But he wanted to push for more answers.

"What happened to my mother?" Why would she write all this stuff about secrets, and needing peace and shit?" "Why are you lying to me?"

"Boy, I'm not going to tell you again to watch how you talk to me!" His father's tone used to tell him a lot; when to get excited when to be calm when to be quiet.

Right now he was immune to it all.

"Tell me what happened to her!" Dhorian screamed.

"Boy, I'll show you to respect me."

Before Dhorian could blink, his father had his hands around his neck. He was choking the fire out of him. Dhorian's sobs cut short when he realized he was running out of air.

"How dare you talk to me like that? Your mother tried to talk to me like that. She tried to take you away from me. I had to show that whore who she was talking to. Like mother like son. Huh? That's how I know for sure your ass is not mine. Too bad it took all of this time for me to see it."

At the mention of his mother, Dhorian found new wind. His father had started to bang his head against the concrete floor, and he could feel himself blacking out. Grabbing at his father and gasping for air, through his haze, Dhorian managed to grab a scalpel, and he closed his eyes and began to slice until he couldn't feel his father's hands around his throat any more. When he felt the pressure release, he jumped up, eyes stinging from the tears and something that got in his eyes. Wiping his eyes with the back of his hand and gulping to fill his lungs with air, Dhorian realized that the growls were coming from him. His hands had blood all over them. Looking around for his father, he saw him slumped on the floor in front of him. Dropping to his knees to check his pulse, Dhorian started to panic as he tried to find it through the bloody gashes on his father's neck and hands. He heard his father cough and flipped him over on his side.

"I'm sorry! I'm so sorry," Dhorian cried out.

"Me too, son," he heard his father say as he watched him take his last breath.

Dhorian grabbed his father's hand and held it to his chest, moaning in agony. He rocked and wailed until the vibration of his cries burned in his throat and the windows showed that it was dusk outside. Dhorian curled up next to his father and wept.

CHAPTER 22

MADISIN

Madisin felt the cold sweat trickle down her nose and onto her lip, but she couldn't wipe away the uncomfortable wetness that was gathering. Her eyes bugged at seeing Paul standing at the opened door of her room. No, not Paul. Even though it stood in the shadows, she could see that the figure was taller and darker, and wearing a wide-brimmed hat that hid the top of his face. It couldn't have been Paul, Madisin reasoned with herself. Paul despised hats because he said they were used to hide insecurities which he always made sure to relish about not having any. If that were the case, then he wouldn't be hiding his little black secret, but this wasn't the time to open up that old wound.

Madisin needed to refocus her energy on other things; like waking up or why when she asked the figure "Who are you?" she barely heard the words leave her mouth.

As soon as she thought she didn't recognize the shadow, it began to look like Tiffany. Madisin hadn't spoken to Tiffany since Tatiana had disappeared on her watch. She didn't know if Tiffany had something to do with her Babygirl being kidnapped. Over the past month and a half Tiffany left at least thirty voicemails on Madisin's home phone and cell. Madisin blocked her within the first week. There was no way in hell she could give that same version of the kidnapping and say that she remembered absolutely nothing after she and Tatiana made it to the car, and still be her friend. Just as quick as the shadows turned into Tiffany, it shifted its shape again to look like the man from the grocery store parking lot. And who the hell knew who or where he was.

The figure began to approach the foot of her bed in an eerie stutter-step from across the room, her nerve endings tingling. Her breathing increased in pace and became louder, and the fear that had risen in her made her tremble. When that fear scratched at her throat and tried to escape as a scream, she only heard silence. Now that she thought about it, everything was too silent. There was dead silence all around her, and this couldn't be. Something in the house should be making noise. There was a leaky faucet in the bathroom outside her door that should have a steady drip. There was an old clock in the hallway that would skip second ticks, but should still be ticking. The man was steadily shuffling closer and closer to the foot of her bed, and even he should be making the old wood floorboards in the house creak.

Madisin had experienced plenty of nightmares in her thirty-two years of living, but this one was becoming too real. No matter how hard Madisin tried, she couldn't wake herself up. She tried to convince herself that a cold sweat and a shadowy figure standing in her usually closed doorway was nothing to fear. The stiffness in Madisin's arms; the soreness of her throat; and the rope she saw tied around each of her ankles made her know otherwise.

The ice-cold splash of water on her face made her sit upright in bed, gasping for air and pulling at the darkness. Madisin couldn't catch her breath because something was still covering her mouth. Flailing her arms and trying to get free, Madisin thought, "Dear God. Jesus help me! Don't let me die."

It was her mother's soft words and a cold rag at the nape of her neck that finally calmed her. She also felt that it was her mother's hand that had covered her mouth.

Gaining her composure and noticing the steely gaze in her mother's eyes, Madisin asked her mother, "What's wrong ma? Everything okay?" The way her mother looked was similar to the way she felt in the nightmare. Madisin gave God a silent prayer of thanks for getting her out of that one.

"Shhhh, girl. I heard something moving round out in the back yard. Your screaming woke me up, and I heard a noise outside the kitchen when I walked by."

Looking at how big her mother's eyes were, and the slugger her mother kept leaned against the back door now at the foot of her bed, "Momma, what's going on?"

Madisin tried to whisper, but her heightened state of awareness at her mother's worried appearance made her whisper come out more like an announcement.

Then gasping, her hand covering her own mouth, "Where's Babygirl?"

Scanning the left and the right of her bed and flipping her covers to peer over and under them frantically. Since Tatiana had been home from the hospital, Madisin had kept her Babygirl by her side. Making sure she kept up with her medication, ate right, and got enough rest to heal properly was a feat within itself. Tatiana had slept in the bed with her every night for the past month. But she wasn't by her side now.

"No, momma! Not again. She's gone." Madisin wailed.

"Shhhh girl. You want to tell them exactly where we are?"

"Them who ma?" Madisin managed to whisper back through her confusion.

Madisin felt like she had woke from one nightmare and into another.

"I think someone is trying to break into the house," her mother whispered.

Panic-stricken, Madisin's next thoughts were about her daughter.

Gripping her mother's hand, terror quaking through her limps, Madisin asked as quietly as she could, "Momma, where is my baby? I got to find Babygirl so we can get out of here."

"You don't remember, do you, baby? She's been wanting to sleep in her bed for a while now and tonight was her first night. Tatiana was in her bed last I checked."

Madisin gulped a sigh of relief and palmed her forehead. She felt her mother's comforting hand on top of hers.

"We'll go get her together. We are not leaving without her. You take this bat. I got another one in the hallway."

Madisin mirrored her mother's hushed finger over her lips and nodded her head in understanding. Throwing the ruffled blanket away from her, Madisin stepped hurriedly across her room and to her makeshift closet. She pulled a thin coat from one of the baskets for Babygirl. And she picked up a pair of sneakers for Babygirl and a pair for herself. Madisin slid her feet as quietly as she could, into her shoes. She motioned to her mother to get behind her. Together, they crept into the darkened hallway and out of her room. The moonlight lit the old shotgun house well enough to see most of the house and if anything was waiting for them in the shadows. Madisin peered to the right, towards the front of the house, bat in hand and ready to swing. She poised herself to bash anything that didn't sound like house settling noises. There was nothing.

Before she could turn to look to the back of the house, she heard a loud crash and a small yelp.

"Babygirl" Madisin and her mother whispered loudly in unison.

This prowler didn't know what they had coming. Staying close to and following the far wall, hand in hand, Madisin and her mother tip-toed past the kitchen and the laundry room to get to the back room where Babygirl slept and where they heard the scream.

As they approached the fuchsia painted door, Madisin heard rustling noises from the other side of the door and then "Mommy!" came out from under the door like it was grabbing her by her throat.

Terrified, Madisin and her mother both gripped their bats tightly and pushed the door open barely touching the knob. Babygirl gave out a shrill scream which made Madisin shriek and her mother do the same. Madisin's screams died down when looking around the room expecting destruction or her Babygirl struggling with the intruder or all other worse case scenarios, but saw none of those things. She handed her bat over to her mother and sat on the bed of her sweat-soaked daughter.

"Oh, mommy. I had a bad, bad dream. There was this man, and he had tied you up and took you away, and I couldn't find you." her Babygirl belted out without being asked, wrapping her arms around her mother.

Even though her daughter's words made her blood turn to ice in her veins, Madisin squeezed her daughter tight, comforting her, and then began to dress her over her nightgown in the jacket and shoes she brought from her room. Still looking around the room, Madisin noticed that Babygirl's Minnie Mouse lamp was in pieces on the floor. She bit her lip and hugged Babygirl tighter to hold back the scream lodged in her throat at the sight of what looked like muddy footprints that lead from Babygirl's window past her mother who stood motionless following her daughter's eyes into the darkened hallway.

CHAPTER 23

VERDELL

Verdell crouched low, out of the streetlight, and ran through the carport into the backyard. He peeked into each window on his way. This job was proving to be one of the most drawn-out, but it was also the going to be the biggest payday he had ever seen. He had almost called his handler to retract his bid on the contract after the blond came in the garage and after the little girl went missing in the grocery store parking lot. His instructions were precise. The job involved killing the woman and the little girl. Verdell felt a little off about it because he had never offed a kid before, at least not directly. But he was being paid for a job, and he never left a job undone.

After the grocery store, he hung back for a while. Hearing that someone had got to the little girl first and kidnapped her, let him know that this lady had more issues than he was coming to bring her. So he laid low and watched her. He thought he had lost the job because the girl was gone. He had followed the mother for weeks looking for an angle to recoup some of his losses by still performing the job in a way that would satisfy his handler, but there was no need for plan B. It was just his luck that the little girl turned up at Brandon Regional. Excited that the opportunity was back in play, Verdell called his handler to confirm the job was still needed and everything was a go.

Seemingly, Verdell had run into luck again when he found the window he was searching for. He slid on his gloves and used his Damascus steel blade to jimmy the side of the screen window. It popped off the frame with no problem and barely a sound. Using the butt of the knife to knock softly at the glass pane, Verdell checked to see if there was any immediate movement in the room. The last thing he wanted was for the surprise to be on him instead of the other way around. As Verdell lifted himself through the window and crept into the dimly lit purple and pink bedroom, his emotions grabbed him at his throat. He remembered being in a girly bedroom similar to this one not that long ago. Verdell shuddered at the memory and forced the contents of his stomach back down his throat. He couldn't think about that now.

It only took him a second to glance around the room and find his target. None of his training could have prepared him for this. A child. Who the hell puts a hit out on a child? Their own child at that. His handler promised that this would be an easy in and out like the others, but seeing the little girl's coconut colored face and bright red coils tangled on top of her head and her long legs splayed across the bed without a care in the world made his heartache. She couldn't have been older than ten, twelve, at the most.

Verdell could have had a baby girl, who would have grown to look something like her. It brought him to a knee at the thought of what he needed to do. He had to get his head in the game, but rising thoughts of Missy and his unborn child made it a lot harder to do that. It took months for the doctors at the camp to rid him of the hallucinations and lurid dreams he had been having but healing his heart wouldn't be so easy. Taking in a deep breath and remembering that this was his way out and how many zeros were behind this job, Verdell shifted his body to stand back to his feet. On his way up, he removed a syringe with a capped needle from the small knapsack on his back. But he was tangled in a cord. Just when he thought he had pulled enough of the cable to create enough slack for him to get his foot out of the noose, *CRASH*.

The loud noise startled him and the little girl. He had to move. Staying low to the floor and on all fours, Verdell scrambled to the door as quietly as he could and looked back to make sure that the little girl hadn't gotten out of the bed. When their eyes met, she screamed, piercing his eardrums, and he quickly opened the door, making sure to close it back and crept swiftly through the darkness into the dimly lit hallway. Slowly creeping down the long corridor of the shotgun house, Verdell stopped short and suddenly when he saw shadows approaching quickly ahead of him. He slipped into the nearest room and pressed his back against the closest wall he could find and sucked in a deep breath. Through the still and quiet air, he heard the excited whispers of what he counted as two women coming down the hallway toward him. He knew the little girl's scream was loud enough to wake someone. He just didn't know who that someone would be.

If there were only the two women, then this should be a piece of cake, and he could have this done in less than twenty minutes. Verdell looked around the room, his eyes adjusted to the darkness, and he realized that he was in the kitchen. Good. That would come in handy. He just had to make his move. He heard the women pass the kitchen and another scream as the room door opened. Women. Verdell shook his head, trying to get the shrill ring out of his ears. He heard what had to be the little girl frantically describing their encounter and then silence.

The air hung around him, and just as he moved to find something in the kitchen to subdue them, he slipped but caught himself before falling. Good thing too or he would have stabbed himself with the poison in the needle. There was only supposed to be one woman and one child, not two women. He would use the time that they were unconscious to figure out what to do with the other one. Looking down at his feet, Verdell saw what he had slipped on and what he saw placed him at a disadvantage. The mud from the yard had followed Verdell into the house. There was no question that his muddy footprints are what had caused the silence in the other room. They knew he was there. Moving swiftly around the kitchen, Verdell saw a wooden block filled with knives. He grabbed the one with the longest handle and pushed the block with the remaining knives into the open garbage can right as he heard a whooshing sound whistling towards him from behind. It was on. Verdell ducked just in time to miss getting his head bashed in with a bat. Staring at the crazed woman in front of him, he almost didn't notice the older woman preparing to swing her bat at his right side. Jumping out of the way, Verdell slashed at the air in front of him to clear his path. Verdell rolled onto his back and into a crouched position that gave him a better visual of his attackers. He thought it strange that he would think of the women as his attackers considering why he was there. But at this moment, he was being attacked and had to do something fast before one of the swinging bats coming towards him connected.

Charging at the older woman, Verdell picked her up by her legs and rammed her into the nearest thing he could find. Dropping the needle in the process, he took a second look to make sure she wasn't getting up before he scrambled to catch the needle rolling under the table. Before he could grab it, he felt a sharp pain seize his right calf. And then his left. The searing pain shot from his legs up to his back. It took mere seconds for Verdell's brain to register that he needed to shift his position or he would be the one dying tonight. Verdell realized it was a bat that was hammering him and not the knife he feared was stabbing him. He thanked God for small favors. Adrenaline pumping, Verdell avoided another hit by rolling toward the table and used the counter to balance his weight. With one hand, he dug the knife deep into the younger woman's leg and left it while he used the other hand to reach the needle. Wailing, the woman backed away withdrawing the knife. But, unlike the older woman, she charged back. Knife in hand, she gave Verdell three slashes across his arm.

Verdell grabbed his arm to try to stifle the burn, "you bitch!" Verdell growled.

Now pissed, he grabbed her arm, squeezing it tight until she dropped the knife. He wrapped her arm around her back and pulled up swiftly, dislocating the woman's shoulder with a pop. She wailed in agony as her arm hung limply by her side. The woman slumped onto the kitchen table, writhing and crying out, "why are you doing this?" Verdell took a moment to catch his breath and survey the damage. The old lady was stirring. He was going to need a crew to clean and lay cover after this one.

"Nanna! Mommy!"

Every head in the kitchen turned to the little girl's shattering voice at the sight of her grandmother and mother hurt and bleeding. She stood in the kitchen doorway like a statue. Verdell wondered how long she had been standing there. Shit! The job was getting to be too drawn out and too messy for Verdell's liking. He needed to put them down and end this. The last thing he needed was screams waking the neighborhood up.

Verdell took the knife that fell on the floor and threw it at the little girl hitting her in her chest. She went down in the doorway without a sound. Both the mother and the grandmother screamed and charged towards him. He caught the older woman by her throat and squeezed. She began coughing for air. With the other hand, he delivered two punches to the younger woman. One to her diaphragm and another to her throat. Only when she hit the floor did he release the older woman. Verdell bent down to look for the needle. He needed it to finish the job. In the next instance, Verdell somehow found himself gasping for air. Damn, these women had moxie. The chokehold became tighter. No matter how Verdell swung the younger woman, she wasn't letting go. He decided to roll her instead. They spun on the ground struggling for the advantage. Before Verdell could take out his Damascus from his belt, the woman stopped moving. The woman stared, eyes fixed on the ceiling. The moonlight was radiating the emptiness in her eyes.

She said to him in a voice as cool as ice, "I know who you are. You were at the store the day my Babygirl went missing. The one from the parking lot."

Verdell stared at the woman in silence. Heavy tears began to stream from her eyes.

"I had a dream that you were coming," she said with a quiet sob. And then her eyes met Verdell's.

The moon made her face look sunken and hollow, but her eyes burned with an eerie yellow that commanded Verdell's attention. Sniffling away her tears, the woman locked eyes with him.

"Please don't let my Babygirl die. Please."

And with her last plea, her body started shaking uncontrollably. Verdell jumped back in surprise. Was she having a seizure? The woman's eyes began to roll back in her head, and her tongue looked as if it was swelling in her mouth. White foam drained from her ears and quickly turned pink with blood.

"Shit! The needle." Verdell moved her trembling body, searching for the needle that he knew had to be the reason for her sudden paralysis and reaction. Her body was flaming hot. She was burning up from the inside. Her body was cooking itself. Lifting her arm, he finally saw why the woman didn't move. There it was, lodged into her shoulder blade. It looked like she landed on the needle and broke it in half but not before being injected with some of the poison first. Suddenly, the woman grabbed his wrist, and he thought he saw Missy's face.

"Missy? Missy baby?"

The blood that drained from the woman's eyes took him back to the burning window. The last night he held Missy. The woman's grip tightened on his wrist. There was no white left in her eyes. She was rapidly blinking and screaming, and all Verdell could see was Missy's face. He struggled to get her off of him, but somehow her grip drained his strength.

Verdell screamed, "No. No." and began dragging his and the woman's body across the floor.

He was trying to escape his pain and the pain tearing away at the woman's face.

She screamed, "My baby. Please save my baby."

Verdell knew the voice wasn't Missy's. But it was Missy's face he saw. This couldn't be happening. It was the biggest job he had. His last one, and he was losing it. What in the hell was going on? He had to get out of here. Verdell pulled his wrist back and moved his legs to kick the woman off him. The heat from her body was burning his wrist through his gloves. He could smell and feel his flesh peeling. On the third kick, she finally let go, and he backed away to the wall.

He heard, "Please. My Babygirl", on her lips as he got up to run away.

Verdell was ready to get out of there. Not ever had he been compelled to leave a job before he had finished, but now he was spooked. Verdell gathered himself and snatched the embedded needle and broken syringe from the woman's wound and darted to leave the kitchen, but not before tripping at the entrance to the kitchen and falling over the old woman and the little girl. Looking at them, he struggled to decide on what his next move should be.

The woman's voice with Missy's face replayed in his head. "Please don't let my Babygirl die."

Verdell pushed the old woman aside. She looked like she wanted to put up a fight to protect the little girl, but Verdell didn't have time for the bullshit. He pulled out his Damascus and showed it to her.

"If you move, if you scream, I can promise you there will be nothing left to protect."

The old woman gulped hard and nodded quickly. Verdell

put his ear to the little girl's mouth and felt her breath on his ear. It was faint, but it was there.

"Hold this." The old woman reached for the steel blade. Verdell quickly pulled it back. "You know I can kill you with my bare hands, right?"

Again, the old woman nodded her head quickly.

"Good."

He handed his steel blade over to her while he rummaged through his bag. The knife he threw into the little girl's chest more than likely pierced her lung, but she was holding on to something. For a family of women, they sure as shit had a lot more resilience than the men he went after. He put his head to her chest.

As he thought, if she didn't get help soon, she was going to drown in her blood. Verdell worked quickly to remove the knife and placed a thin tube into the wound, bringing air into her chest cavity and pushing the blood out of her lungs. He poked a hole in the gauze pad he kept in his bag in case he ever ran into trouble and used duct tape to secure it tightly to her chest. He grabbed his Damascus back from the old woman, who quickly rushed to her granddaughter's side.

"Take her far away from here and find somewhere else to start over. This dressing should give you about an hour before you have to stop and get her treated at a hospital." Before he would let the woman thank him, he made sure to let her know, "Next time, I will finish the job."

She grabbed the little girl tightly to her bosom instead of trying to thank him this time.

On his way out the backdoor, Verdell yelled, "you have precisely four minutes and thirty seconds to leave the property before this house burns to the ground."

*

Verdell left the house, clouded. It was the first time in close to a year that he had not finished a job.

"Shit, shit, shit, shit, shit, shit, shit!" Verdell yelled as he hit the steering wheel over and over again.

In the dark alley, where he sat, the rain fell on his windshield and provided cover. His screams and his tears surged through his body and surrounded him in the space. Tonight he saw his love. He saw Missy's face, and it almost cost him his life. Tonight would be the second time Verdell found himself punished for loving her. But not anymore. Tonight's slip up would be his last. Verdell put his Charger in drive and sped off into the night. He heard the blast in the distance as he merged on to I-4 from 275 South.

"Goodbye and good riddance."

EPILOGUE:

DHORIAN

Dhorian woke up to what felt like a hammer knocking against his skull. His vision was blurred, and he didn't recognize his surroundings.

"Mr. Hamilton. Mr. Hamilton. Are you up?"

Dhorian's throat was so dry. He couldn't have answered if he wanted to. He heard several voices.

"Mr. Christen. Mr. Christen, he is up."

Mr. Christen? He remembered going home, but what was Mr. Christen doing here?

"Dhorian. Dhorian, son? How are you feeling? A little woozy?"

He recognized Mr. Christen's voice, but he couldn't open his eyes. They hurt too badly.

"Maria, would you bring him some water please?" "Dhorian. It's okay if you're not feeling like yourself. I had my family physician give you a mild sedative. You've been out for a few days."

Dhorian sipped the cold water. It singed his blistered throat. He coughed.

"I only have a few minutes before you probably pass out again. So I need you to try and focus okay. I found you at your father's funeral home. When you didn't come back after lunch, I thought you gave up on me, and I tried to call your father. When your father didn't pick up, I got worried. I mean he's like old reliable. He always picks up. Barry and I drove by your house, and when you weren't there, we went around back to the funeral home to check on things. We found you and your father in the downstairs room. It looked like a robbery gone wrong. You got banged up pretty good, but I'm sorry to say your father didn't make it."

Confusion clouded Dhorian's mind. He couldn't understand. A robbery? What was Mr. Christen talking about? He had to be mistaken. Dhorian drank more water and tried to ask a question, but just ended up spitting up the water.

"Hey, hey, hey, don't overexert yourself. And don't worry about a thing. Barry and I took care of everything."

Dhorian willed his eyes to open. His head was swirling. His father didn't make it. He thought he remembered that.

"My fault," Dhorian managed to mumble.

"No, it's not your fault. These things happen. No need to blame yourself. You just work on getting better."

Dhorian felt the weight shift on the bed as Mr. Christen stood.

"Oh and Barry found what looked to be your mother's diary and had it cleaned for you. It's on the nightstand next to your bed whenever you're ready for it."

Hearing about his mother's diary made Dhorian sit straight up in bed. He forced his vision clear as he saw Mr. Christen leave the room before he passed out again.

EPILOGUE:

PAUL

Sitting at dinner with his wife, his daughter, and his mother-in-law, Paul was trying his best to be engaged. He knew he had been acting a little distant for the past few months, and this dinner was his last resort at restoring normalcy to their household. Sandra would not stop hovering over him after meetings and during doctor's visits and when they went to bed at night, practically begging him to tell her what was wrong with him. And it was taking everything in him, not to say *"You. You are what's wrong with me."* Granted it would have been insulting to do so seeing how attentive she had been to him during his time of need, but it would have also been inaccurate to say that only Sandra was what was wrong with him.

The phone rang. Sandra's neck snapped her head in his direction. He saw the glare in her eyes, and he knew not to move. Paul chose to ignore the phone altogether and continued his conversation with his daughter about the fifth grade bully in school who finally got in trouble for beating up a little kid.

"Oh, and you had to see it, daddy. You just had to be there." Christina rattled on and on. And honestly, he didn't mind.

Working as he did and recovering from the transplant, he often missed these intimate moments with his daughter and didn't want to take them for granted considering that she would be the only daughter he would regrettably be spending time with according to his last fall out with Madisin. The shrill ringing continued incessantly.

"For God's sake, Paul go ahead and answer it." He saw the pink hue in his wife's face slowly growing red.

Not eager to give in to her mood, Paul threw his hands up casually and said: "Oh Madisin will get it."

He caught himself off guard. Did he just say that? Did Sandra hear him say that? The air around the table had grown still and hot. It was as if everyone had gasped the coolness out of the air at the same time. He hadn't heard from Madisin since the park and Barry said he was still working on locating her, so he wasn't sure why at this present moment, her name was what came out.

Clearing his throat and backing away from the table, Paul announced, louder than his last statement, "I'll get it." as if that would erase the fact that he called out the name of his secretary who had been considered MIA for the past four months. Paul walked tall to the phone.

"Hello. Paul Christen speaking." There was dead silence on the other end.

"It's done," the voice said.

"Excuse me?" Paul placed his index finger in his ear to ensure he was hearing the speaker clearly. "Done. What's done?" Paul had no idea what the caller was referring to, but there was a steely pain in the pit of his stomach. There was a cold laugh on the other end.

"This is Paul Christen, correct?"

"Yes, yes, this is Paul Christen."

"Well, I'm only going to give you more detail because you paid so well for the job."

"Job? What job?" Paul questioned in a panic. The caller laughed again.

"You right. What job?" the man said sinisterly.

Paul's palms were sweaty. He covered his mouth with his hand to distort some of what he knew his family had tried to eavesdrop.

"You say I paid you so well, tell me what exactly it is you did so I can make sure that you did a job worthy of the full payment."

The caller humphed. "Well I've already been paid in full, but if you want to hear all the details…"

Paul now irritated, "yes. Yes. Tell me the details please." The other line went silent again. "Hello. Hello."

"Stop yelling. I'm here. I'm here. Look, I don't know if you are Mr. Paul Christen, so I won't tell you everything. But what I can say is your little problem, the little girl and her mother are no longer problems."

"What? What do you mean, problem? What girl and her mother?"

"Man, you are getting a little excited over a job you requested and paid half up front for, don't you think?"

"Listen here you crook. If you are trying to blackmail me, it will not work because I have no idea who or what you are talking about." Paul heard his voice echo through the quiet kitchen. He guessed that he was given privacy to handle his call. He knew Sandra would be on his ass about this later. But first he needed to deal with this caller, and he was getting impatient. He heard crazed laughter coming from the receiver. "What is so damn funny?"

"I just got the text back from my handler. I got the name of the woman and child I told you about earlier. I work indirectly for you, sir. I am no crook. I usually don't deliver details or names. Only results. But it seems like you were left out of the deal, so let me do you a favor and open a window for you."

"Yeah, okay. Well, who are they?" Paul responded now irritated.

"Madisin and Tatiana Foster were executed last night at 22:45 at their home residence at the request and payment of Mr. Paul Christen to the sum of three hundred and seventy-five thousand dollars to be paid half upfront and the remainder upon confirmation and completion of said assignment. Now, you have a good night, Mr. Paul Christen." The line went dead.

Paul's throat was dry. He held the phone in his hands until

the uncontrollable shaking made him drop the receiver. Paul hadn't realized he was bawling until Barry arrived to pick him up off the floor. Paul's nostrils and throat were so inflamed from his screeching cries that it was hard for him to breath, but he had to know why.

He stopped Barry from dragging him to his office and in a raspy voice, asked the one question that had plagued him since he heard the news, "Why Barry? Why?"

Barry looked at him straight on and with no pity, "Don't worry friend, I found out all I needed to know."

EPILOGUE:

VERDELL

Verdell sat on the eighth step from the top, silencer on, light focused on his father's chest. If he didn't know any better, he would've thought that his father had been drunk and asleep on the same couch he left him on years ago. From where he sat, he could see all of the downstairs except for the kitchen. Not much had changed in the time that Verdell was away. The house still had an old damp smell. Most likely from pipes that still needed fixing. The furniture cloth had a few new holes in the couches, and the beige on it looked more like brown shit stains than geometrical art designs artistically positioned within the blue squares. His mother had once told him that secrets could eat and devour a person's soul and everything good around them if given a chance. Looking around the old house in disgust, Verdell wondered what secrets his father had let fester.

Verdell had been waiting since 10:00 PM for his father to wake up, but it was now 3:00 AM, and he still hadn't moved from that spot. Snoring like a bear, and living in filth. Verdell had been racking his brain. What kind of man would be okay living like this? What kind of man would purposely destroy everything his wife worked so hard for them to have? What kind of father would not only let his son stay in jail for a crime he didn't commit but would act like he didn't exist? Even though he was nineteen at the time of his arrest, Verdell understood now that he was still only just a kid. With all that time on his hands, Verdell rationalized that all the pain and brutality and other shit that he had lived through was his father's fault. He was a selfish ass snake who had let his wife die, and left his son for dead. Verdell had seen places for nasty motherfuckers like him, and Verdell couldn't wait for his father to wake so he could show him exactly where. Live and in color.

Just for shits and giggles, he closed all of the windows and turned on the A/C in the old house when he first arrived. Not only to clear out the disgusting mold smell but to help wake his father up. He knew having the A/C on below 80 degrees Fahrenheit in the house was a pet peeve for his father. Verdell also knew that sooner or later, the cold air would have him popping out of his sleep like a jack in the box. He could have done it the quick way, but he enjoyed this little game. Every hour he would lower the thermostat 5 degrees. The change from 84 to 59 even had him sliding on his leather gloves sooner than he planned.

Verdell had killed more people than he could count over the last four months. The decision to kill his father now or let his sorry ass live until the next time he got the urge to kill him had Verdell torn. His phone vibrated in his pocket looking at the caller id, Verdell knew he had to take the call. Answering the phone, voice low but steady, "Yo, it's Vee. What up?" He listened intently and looked down at his watch. "Okay, I'm in the West. I can be there in twenty minutes." Before the caller had the chance to hang up, Verdell stopped, "Listen, tell them I need to have my money on time for this one too man." And then he abruptly hung up. Verdell walked down the stairs and shook his head, "Count yourself lucky old man," he whispered to his father, shaking the pistol in his direction as he walked towards the front door to leave. Before he closed the door behind him, Verdell took one last look over his shoulder and back at his childhood. He aimed at his father again, this time pulling the trigger twice and then closed the door behind him. What was done was done. He would be better off left for dead. "Goodbye, old man. And good riddance."

A THANK YOU AND A SNEAK PEEK

By way of a thank you for reading *Requiem - Origins* I'm thrilled to be able to share with you the first chapter of the second book in the *Requiem* series: *Exposed*.

Happy reading!
Taveyah LaShay

Chapter 1

VERDELL

Verdell sat idle in his father's driveway, captured by the notification that popped up on his smartphone.
Police Investigate Decapitation After Temple Terrace Man Found Dead
Hillsborough County, Florida – A man was found dead, decapitated, with full-body trauma inside an empty warehouse in Temple Terrace on Harney Road on February 28 at 4:55 p.m., according to the Hillsborough County Sheriff's Office. Deputies have ruled this a homicide and believe the horrifying murder was not a random act.
The Hillsborough County Sheriff's Office asks anyone with information about the death to contact (813) 777-9311. Sheriff Dunn said that all information is essential information. No detail is too small to report. Anyone can

call in tips anonymously to Crime Stoppers.
Police have not released the victim's identity.

A grin spread across Verdell's face as he skimmed the breaking news story. The news notifications helped him keep an eye on how much information the police were willing to reveal. Verdell laughed again as he read that same story a third time. To most people, laughing at something so horrible would constitute insanity, but for Verdell, it was just business. As he got out of his car and grabbed his belongings, Verdell shook his head. He was privy to something the police were not. No one would be calling the tip line to help solve this one. He made sure of that when he disposed of the body.

*

"Hey, Pops. How your legs feeling today?" Verdell asked as he laid his laundry, pressed and starched, fresh from the cleaners, across the new oversized chair in his father's living room.

Verdell Sr., his father, pushed himself back and swayed forth in an old Rocker and Glider chair.

If Verdell was going to continue to stay there, the house needed an upgrade. And social security sure as hell was not paying for luxuries.

"I'm doing as well as I can be, son. You know this plastic keeps me stiff sometimes. But I won't complain." His father grunted and chuckled lightheartedly, tapping his cane against his prosthetic legs.

Verdell stared at his father blankly before bursting into

laughter, a little harder than he should have. His father's look of disgust let him know that he was a little overzealous with that last chuckle, but Verdell shrugged it off. Living without legs was considered a blessing in his father's situation. The old coot should have lost his life.

"Hell, I don't see what you standing over there, snickering about. You over there with both your legs and ain't got the good sense God gave you to not laugh at those who are suffering."

Verdell watched, lip curled into a scowl, as his father used a cane to balance his weight and get up from the chair. Verdell Sr. slid prosthetic feet into his torn old house shoes and shuffled towards the kitchen, mumbling under his breath.

"I don't know why the hell you would ask me just to make fun of me. Something ain't right with that shit there. Not right at all."

Verdell made a mental note to aim higher, possibly for the neck or the head, the next time he felt the extreme urgency to off his father. Verdell hawked his throat and sucked his teeth before following his old man into the kitchen.

Standing at the door, Verdell already knew the answer but figured he would ask, "Did you eat today?"

"What you ask me that for? You going to laugh at me for starving too?" his father asked, full of sarcasm.

Sorting out pots and pans, Verdell prepared to cook a quick dinner of corned beef, rice, and cabbage before he left for the night. "Pops, why all the sarcasm? I asked because I care. I would think that you would have pulled yourself together by now and realized there are better ways to die than starvation."

If feeling sorry for himself was the only sentiment his father gained after being shot and having both of his legs amputated, it was a hell of an improvement. Who knew it would take having his legs blown off to get a little emotion out of him? Maybe if his father had gained a little perspective after they lost his mother, then they would not be here.

Thoughts about losing his mother made Verdell's blood boil, despite reaching into the cold fridge to grab the cabbage and the celery. Verdell had to get a grip on his anger before he ruined everything again.

*

Eight years ago, Verdell shot his father, not once but twice. No matter how justified his anger, it was not an authorized hit. Verdell's job description had always included maintaining self-control as a priority. It was what separated his class from the mongrels. Therefore, his emotional slip-up, howbeit not murder, was still punishable.

When Verdell shot his father, he thought he had walked away from his childhood home for the last time. He would never have expected to be here now, taking care of a man he once blamed for all of the horrible shit that ever happened to him since his mother passed. Maybe he still held him responsible.

After the emotional drain of leaving his father for dead and the gory nature of his assignments in the days leading up to that heated decision, Verdell wanted to give himself a semi-retirement gift. Somewhere peaceful, he could dress his physical and mental wounds, maybe eat a few tasty meals, and take a few ladies for a wild ride. His search for peace led him to a Craigslist ad for a 2.7 acre property with split level home with three bedrooms, three full baths, a barn, and a natural lake in Thonotosassa. It was the perfect location for him to get away when he was not on assignment. Verdell emailed the contact, making sure to tell them he could pay in cash. Not to his surprise, he received a response within minutes, asking when he would be available to see the property.

Verdell checked with all of his sources to make sure the listing was legit. Verdell waited until his connections in the city's Commissioners' office signed off before happily agreeing to set up his walkthrough for the next evening.

The property was more than he could have ever imagined. The pictures were no match for what stood before him. Verdell declined to see the barn and the rest of the land after viewing the main house. Garden jet tubs, marble in the wet areas and main walkways, and plush carpeting in all the rooms. He had to act fast. He felt like he would lose it to another buyer if he did not make an offer now. Verdell could not believe a place like this was still available. And it was going to be his. He offered fifteen percent below the asking price, and it only took the realtor twenty minutes and one question to get his offer accepted. The owner wanted cash. Who would pass up two hundred seventy five thousand dollars cash? Surely not anyone he knew. There was only one problem. Verdell hid his payouts from each job in different accounts. Sometimes, it was hard for him to recall where his handler routed the funds.

The amount of money he accumulated was always a surprise to him. And as long as it kept growing, there were no issues. Verdell chose to live out of his newly acquired 2008 Dodge Challenger and had spent next to nothing since he started wet working. That was one of the perks of the job he loved. It paid for itself. The premium he received for completing each assignment was more like a bonus.

*

Verdell excused himself from the realtor to go outside and check his balance and make the transfer in private. As soon as his foot hit the driveway, he found himself gasping for air as they bagged him.

Verdell began to panic and fought his attackers. He could tell the bag did not have many holes because he felt himself beginning to pass out from the lack of oxygen coming through the small holes in the sack.

Thoughts quickly ran through his head about who could have grabbed him. Who could have known where he would be and catch him off his game? *Could it have been Donnie Belasco's people?* Verdell ruled them out because he had not heard any fake ass Boston accents or smelled any weird combination of basil and cinnamon men's body spray. *How about the guy that had his side piece and his daughter whacked? No. That guy was a fucking sociopath and definitely would have foolishly announced his plan to bag me before paying his stooges to execute me.*

Thoughts about sparing the daughter after murdering her mother made Verdell's chest tighten. He gasped for air, trying to release the tension, but only found himself closer to unconsciousness. He had to stay focused. Verdell realized if he was not dead, the best thing he could do was sit back and enjoy the ride. Verdell breathed in deep and exhaled. Performing that task alone let him know that there was a chance he would make it out of this snatch and grab alive.

Verdell woke up in what he remembered as the diagnostic room. While inside, they showed him pictures of his father airlifted and arriving at Tampa General Hospital. He had not bled out from his bullet wounds. Verdell did not get a chance to explain his botched attempt at revenge. The Camp had Verdell gagged, bare from his waist up, strung upside down, and dipped his entire trigger arm from shoulder to fingertips in concentrated hydrochloric acid. Verdell had to keep his head craned and tried his best to keep it from flailing, despite the convulsions of agony that rippled through his body. They would have to kill him if they wanted him dead. He was not going to dip his head in the acid for them.

Verdell had never felt that type of debilitating pain in his life. He just knew that he would see the bone when they pulled his arm out of the vat. The smell was unbearable. He threw up twice and caught a crick in his neck from trying to stay stiff enough to avoid the acid that was dangerously close to his skull. Burning hair mixed with the smell of dying flesh had Verdell extremely nauseous. To Verdell's surprise, he did not see the bone, but his skin appeared melted into the muscle. He could not remember if he passed out from the pain or the sight of his arm disintegrating right before his eyes.

They tortured and beat Verdell into a haze for days. When he woke up, the fog was so heavy; he could not recall if his torment lasted days or weeks. He was in a dingy two star motel off Fletcher and Nebraska with his arm wrapped in gauze when he came to. Next to him, the number of an orthodontist to replace missing teeth, a manila envelope, and a briefcase holding five hundred twenty five thousand dollars. On the dirt-smudged mirror was a sticky note that said, "If your simple ass didn't know before, now you know who the hell gives the orders, and it sure as hell ain't you. Lay low. We'll call you when we need you."

It took Verdell three full months to heal from his injuries and the surgery on his mouth. He needed to get a sleeve to cover the scar tissue on his arm. He had learned his lesson. The Camp made it clear their position on unauthorized hits. He understood.

Fortunately for him, when he was out of commission, no one had bought the Thonotosassa property. Verdell knew the realtor had a thing for him when they first met, and sure enough, when he called, she was anxious to meet him and go over the purchase contract. Verdell was more than happy to oblige. When he gave her the two hundred seventy five thousand dollars for the property and another fifteen thousand for herself, she had no problem helping him warm the house up. His only catch, she had to do everything in panties, only. Verdell had finally bought his peace.

*

Closing the refrigerator door, Verdell looked at his arm as a reminder of his lack of discipline. He would not dare risk going down that road again. At the oddest moments, the smell of burnt skin and hair still haunted him. Especially in times like these, when he felt his sorry ass father had many more secrets to be punished for.

ABOUT THE AUTHOR

Taveyah LaShay is an author residing in Brandon, Florida and is behind *Requiem: Origins*, the first book in a dramatic thriller trilogy series.

The second book in the series - *Requiem: Exposed* - is now available on Amazon.

You can visit Taveyah online at **www.taveyahlashay.com** or on Facebook, Instagram, or Twitter (@TaveyahWrites).

www.ingramcontent.com/pod-product-compliance
Lightning Source LLC
Chambersburg PA
CBHW020405080526
44584CB00014B/1183